HOW TO DO
CHRISTMAS FLORALS
IF YOU THINK YOU CAN'T

The publisher and designer wish to thank the following companies for providing materials used in this publication:

- **Adhesive Technologies, Inc.** for low temperature Craft and Floral Pro™ Glue gun and sticks
- **American Oak Preserving Co.** for dried and preserved flowers and greenery
- **B.B. World Corp.** for miniature silk flowers and latex berries
- **C.M. Offray & Son, Inc.** for ribbon
- **Crisa Corp.** for glass vase
- **Decorator & Craft Company** for ornaments
- **Delta Color Accents™** for the Gold Highlighter™
- **Design Master® Color Tool, Inc.** for floral spray paints and tints
- **Duncan** for the Icicle Snow™
- **Hot Off The Press, Inc.** for the Paper Pizazz™ Christmas paper
- **International Flower Imports, Inc.** for preserved greenery
- **Lion Ribbon Co., Inc.** for ribbon
- **Luzon Imports** for all TWIGS™ vine wreaths and the birdhouse
- **Modern Forge** for the hurricane lamp
- **MPR Associates, Inc.** for paper ribbon
- **Schusters Of Texas, Inc.** for dried and preserved flowers, greenery and fruit
- **Select Farms, Ltd.** for the preserved salal wreath
- **Teter's Floral Products, Inc.** for silk flowers
- **Wang's International, Inc.** for silk flowers, grapes, ornaments, vinyl greens, baskets, candle cups, picks, angels, bead garlands, gold plastic coral, sleigh, chair and angel
- **Wimpole Street Creations, Inc.** for doilies
- **Winward Silks** for silk and latex flowers and berries

About the Designer:

Anne-Marie Spencer lives in Oregon with her best friend, Laurence, and is the in-house floral designer for Hot Off The Press. Her background includes creating floral designs for many national catalogs as well as traveling abroad to design basketware. Hot Off The Press is happy to have Anne-Marie on our team and delighted to share her talents with you. As you might guess, Anne-Marie is already hard at work on more floral books.

Dedicated with all my love to my darling Laurence, whose compassion, strength and encouragement help make my life complete.

Candles and fires in fireplaces are common during the holidays—in fact, many of the projects in this book feature arrangements with candles. However, both fresh and artificial floral materials are flamable and are dangerous if left unattended near an open flame. Please be careful.

Production Credits:

Project editor: Tara Choate, Katie Hacker, Lori Stephens
Technical editor: LeNae Gerig, Terry Dolney
Photographer: Susannah Roth, Kevin Laubacher
Graphic designers: Sally Clarke, Jacie Pete, Susan Shea
Digital imagers: Michael Kincaid, Larry Seith
Editors: Teresa Nelson, Tom Muir

published by  P.O. Box 55595
Little Rock, Arkansas 72215

produced by

Library of Congress #97-73900
Hardcover ISBN 0-8487-4114-5
Softcover ISBN 1-57486-073-9

HOW TO DO
CHRISTMAS FLORALS
IF YOU THINK YOU CAN'T

TABLE OF CONTENTS

Great GARLANDS & Sensational SWAGS

Treasured Trims for the Tree

Fabulous & Fresh Boughs & Bows

Fast, Easy & FESTIVE

Identification of Floral Materials

Walking into a floral department in a craft store can be very overwhelming if you aren't prepared for what you'll see or if you're not sure of what you need. Our list of materials needed for each project should help, but what if you don't know the difference between a latex and a silk flower? This section has photos of the most commonly used materials in flower-arranging with a short explanation of their properties. While not every store carries every stem used in the book, knowledge of what you're searching for will help should you need to substitute stems.

Fluff the silk flower, pine or fir stems before using them in a project. Garlands are usually sold coiled, so the sprigs are mashed close to the main stem. Bend the stems and sprigs to curve naturally. If the leaves are wired, shape them to extend among the blossoms or fruit. On pine or fir wreaths, shape each sprig to extend as desired; usually angling them all one direction, either clockwise or counter-clockwise around the wreath, provides the most natural look. Grape stems usually have wired tendrils which may be stretched out of shape. Wrap the tendrils around a round pen, remove the pen and slightly stretch the coil for a natural look.

Polysilk Flowers

Because "silk" flowers aren't actually made from silk, but from polyester, they hold their shapes well; some are actually weatherproof. In recent years the quality of polysilks has greatly improved, with more realistic flowers being created. Natural colors are used, with shading or veining in the petals to make them more botanically correct.

"Dried-Silk" Flowers

These are polysilk flowers, but with curled edges which make them look dried.

Delores Ruzicka, a designer in Nebraska, has discovered a method of turning regular poly-silks into dried silks which she calls "flower zap-ping." Hold the flower by the stem in one hand; direct the heat from a heat gun or paint stripper onto the petals and leaves, being very careful not to burn yourself. Begin on a low temperature setting to acquaint yourself with the process.

Zapping stems of polysilk leaves can make them more realistic. Orange, yellow and brown autumn leaves, as well as regular green leaves, once zapped, can become very attrac-tive additions to floral designs.

Hand-Wrapped Flowers

Most elegant silk and parchment flowers are actually hand-wrapped, meaning they're assembled by hand and the stems are wrapped with floral tape. Their stems can be hard to cut, because the flowers and leaves are on separate wire stems which are wrapped together onto a heavier wire.

Of course, the more effort put into producing the flowers, the more expensive they become. However, a design using high-quality, realistic flowers can be enjoyed much longer than the inexpensive polysilks; they will be in style longer with their colors spanning more seasons.

Foam Flowers

Recently developed foam flowers are constructed of high-density, very thin foam. Usually, as is the case with the flowers shown, the leaves or thicker parts of the flowers are foam with the blossom being polysilk. The results are blossoms and leaves which are extremely realistic to view and to touch.

In an effort to make silk flowers more botanically correct and to add visual interest to arrangements, manufacturers also create flowers with bulbs and roots attached. The only limitation to using these is they must be left intact, making it difficult to achieve varying heights in the design. While being wonderful to use, they also add another level of realism.

Fabric Flowers

Non-woven fabric is used to make these flowers. It is cut and shaped into petals, which are then hand-wrapped together. The leaves usually include wires to shape them, and flower petals are shaded for more realism. Veins and ridges pressed into the petals as well as muted colors achieved in the finishing process result in a very upscale look.

Latex Flowers

Parchment and silk flowers that have a cool, rubbery feel have been dipped in latex. They're realistic to touch and add an elegant look to an arrangement.

Keep latex flowers away from heat as the latex can soften and become sticky. Store in a cool, dry place.

Silk Bushes

These are available in many configurations, as flowering plants or as greenery with varying numbers of branches attached to one main stem. The branches may vary in length on one stem, making the bush look realistic. Some bushes include more than one type of flower or plant. These are fun to work with, since the colors are already coordinated for you—plus they may be less expensive to use than individual stems! Of course the more branches on a plant stem, the more expensive it becomes. And with more branches to work with, a fuller, lusher design can be made. To use a bush, either insert it as a plant in a design, or cut the branches off the main stem and insert individually. Sprigs may also be cut off each branch and attached to a base.

Flowering Vines & Garlands

Different types of flowers and plants come as long vines. They vary in lengths from 30" to 9 feet and are convenient if a long garland is required.

Garlands can be a base for additional materials such as dried or silk flowers, allowing the creation of some unique vines. Dip the flower stem ends in hot glue and insert them among the garland leaves or flowers, making sure they are glued to the main garland stem. Or wire flower stems to a long floral garland.

Pine or Fir Garlands

PVC or vinyl pine or fir garlands commonly come in 9-foot lengths and are very versatile. They can be cut into shorter lengths and wired to baskets, wreaths or other bases.

It can be quicker and easier to use a garland than individual pine stems for designing. A pine garland wired to a grapevine wreath is a great start for a Christmas design. Or, if pine stems are needed but none are on hand, make them by cutting 8–12-sprig sections of pine garland and wiring each to a long wood pick.

To cut a garland, spread apart the individual sprigs and cut through the heavy binding wires; twist the cut wire ends together to secure the sprigs nearest the ends.

Picks

Floral picks are short stems of clustered items. Holiday picks may include berries, cones, silk leaves, packages, ornaments, pine sprigs and more. Short (4"–7" tall) stems of flowers, fruit or greenery are also called picks. Smaller flower picks generally include 1–3 blossoms with several leaves per stem. Greenery picks can be small plants, such as violets, or just leaves on a stem; these look especially nice clustered in a design.

While picks can be effective inserted as stems, they can also be cut into individual components. Attach each to a wood pick, then insert into the design in a scattered pattern.

Artificial Fruits & Vegetables

Important elements in floral designing, these are available in polysilk, vinyl, or latex, and can be attached directly to the design, among the materials. If a pick or stem is needed on the fruit or vegetable for insertion, glue or wire one to the bottom or to a hidden area of the piece.

Berry Stems

Stems of berries, whether smooth or textured (like blackberries) have remained popular, adding interest or becoming fillers in a design. Intricate berry stems with vines and branches attached are also available. They can look good enough to eat and add color, shine, and unique textures to arrangements.

Berries are available as picks, on stems or as vines. They come with or without leaves and can even be found mixed in with flowers or greenery on the same stem. Berries are fun to include in woodsy designs, adding a wild, natural look.

Pods & Mushrooms

It's easy to find many varieties of pods with a wide range of sizes, colors and textures. Dried tree fungus, also known as dried sponge mushrooms, are a realistic addition to the woodsy, natural look. Mushrooms and pods come attached to wired stems or wood picks, making them easy to use.

canella

eskira pod

bell cup

jacaranda pod

okra pod

sponge mushroom

Cones

Different types of cones are available for purchase, many with heavy stems attached (some have even been cut apart to resemble flowers). Or you can collect your own cones to use in projects.

Always use fresh cones; if they crumble in your hands, they are too old. If they've been collected from trees, rinse them under running water to remove dust and debris, then bake on a

cookie sheet at 225° for one hour to open the petals again. Cones can be glued, wired or inserted directly into a project, depending on the look wanted and how they are prepared.

Mosses

Mosses are most often used to cover the mechanics of an arrangement, such as foam, wire or glue. The moss in a design is chosen for its color or texture and is secured with U-shaped floral pins or with glue.

Natural Spanish moss is gray; if a soft, neutral look is desired, it works nicely. A product called gray American Moss® imitates Spanish moss but is actually excelsior; it's cleaner to use, with nearly the same effect. Other colors are available in American Moss®, such as green and brown, which are useful for other looks. Sphagnum moss, also known as sheet moss, is used when a green "growing" look is needed. It comes packaged in layers or in sheets to be peeled apart as needed. Reindeer moss is gray with a unique texture that looks great when it can be seen as part of the design. It's available dried or preserved; the dried version is very brittle, whereas the preserved moss is softer. Mood moss is a very thick green moss and is effectively used in designs where the moss is visible as an important component. It has depth, is firm and is easy to work with, especially on larger projects.

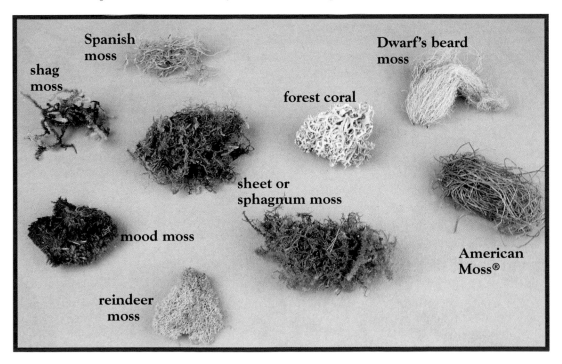

Other more unusual mosses and lichens are available to use in floral design, including forest coral, dwarf's beard and shag moss. All have unique properties and appearances, yet, if one is unavailable, any moss or lichen of similar color and texture can be used as a substitute. All enhance the natural look and feeling of a design, giving each a "back-to nature" appearance.

Tools, Supplies & Putting It All Together

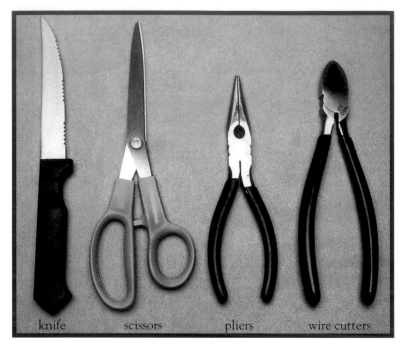

knife   scissors   pliers   wire cutters

The following pages include explanations and photos of all kinds of floral tools and supplies. Sometimes it's difficult to know just which supplies are really needed to complete a project; this information should eliminate some of the confusion and make it easier to decide what is needed and when. Included are some tips for using certain supplies, too.

Tools

A sharp serrated knife, scissors, needle-nose pliers, and heavy-duty wire cutters are valuable tools in dried and silk floral work. The wire cutters need to be sturdy enough to cut through the heavy stems of hand-wrapped silks. Use the pliers to twist wires together, saving tender hands and fingernails. The knife is used to trim floral foam to fit a base. Scissors should be sharp enough to cut ribbons, and shouldn't be used to cut wire, which will nick and dull the blades.

Wires

(A) Wires are measured by gauge—the smaller the number, the heavier the wire. 18–20 gauge wire is used to lengthen or strengthen flower stems (see "Floral Tape," page 14). 22–24 gauge wire is a nice weight for bows or loop hangers. 30-gauge wire is very fine and can be used to attach stems to bases and to secure ribbon loops. (B) Paddle wire is fine- to medium-weight wire rolled onto a wooden paddle and is used whenever a continuous length is needed.

(C) Cloth-covered wires come in either green or white. Green wires resemble flower stems and blend in well with designs. The white wire is useful when doing bridal work. Both are available in stem weight as well as lighter weights for securing items together.

(D) Chenille stems can be used instead of wire to secure bows. Because of their fuzziness, they don't slip as easily—and because of their wide range of colors, they can be matched to the ribbon.

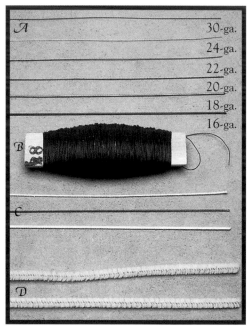

A   30-ga.
24-ga.
22-ga.
20-ga.
18-ga.
16-ga.

B

C

D

Making Wire Loop and U-Pin Hangers

First decide the best placement for a hanger so the project hangs correctly (some projects, such as a garland, will require more than one hanger). Insert a 6"–10" length of 24-gauge wire into the back of the base (or among the vines of a wreath). Bring the end back out and twist both ends together, forming a loop. If the object is solid and a wire can't be inserted, make a wire loop first and hot glue it to the back. (White wire was used here for visibility.)

An easy hanger for a straw or foam wreath can be made by bending the ends of a U-shaped floral pin back and inserting them into the wreath. For extra strength, secure the U-pin with hot glue.

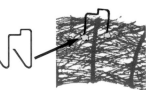

Glues

Tacky craft glue effectively secures stems in floral foam. Dip the cut stem into glue, then insert it into the project. Gluing keeps stems from twisting in or dislodging from the foam, ruining established design lines.

Hot or low temperature glue guns are handy for floral designing. The low temperature gun is safer, but not as secure as hot glue when used on items preserved with glycerine. Apply glue to the stem end, then insert it into foam or onto the base. Hold the item for a moment until the glue sets. Glue sticks are available in different formulas; make sure you use the correct stick for the job and the gun.

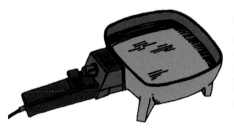

Glue pans, which hold a pool of melted glue at a constant temperature, are useful when you have a lot of gluing to do, since they let you keep one hand free by allowing you to dip the stems.

Floral Foam

Floral foam is available in two types: fresh or "wet" foam and dry foam. Wet foam should be used only for fresh flowers. Because it is made to soak up water and hold it for the fresh stems, it's too soft for dried and silk arrangements. Dry foam, designed to be used with silk and dried flowers, is firmer and holds stems more securely.

To prepare dry foam prior to attaching it to a base, use a serrated knife to cut it to size—trim away as much as possible, leaving a smaller area to be concealed. Cut the corners down to make it fit; if placed in a container, trim it to match the container with 1" extending above the rim. If the foam is to fit into a wreath, be sure to trim away enough so the foam fits snugly against the inner side.

Use the knife to round the top edges and corners of the foam. This will make it easier to cover with moss or excelsior and make the "ground" where the stems are inserted look more natural. Do not cut away so much of the foam that it no longer extends the correct amount above the rim of the container. It's much easier to achieve a natural, growing look in an arrangement if you're able to insert stems into the foam sides to extend parallel with the table. Usually no more than 1" needs to extend above the rim to achieve this effect.

To attach floral foam to a base, glue or wire it in place. To wire it, first cover an area on the top of the foam with a strip of moss or excelsior, then wrap a 30-gauge wire length over the foam and around the base, twisting the ends at the back to secure. The moss prevents the wire from pulling through the foam.

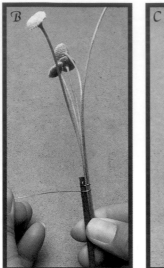

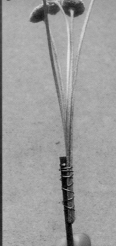

Wood Picks

These add length or strength to floral items. To add a wired wood pick to a cluster of dried flowers:

(A) Position the flowers in the cluster at varying heights, then cut the stems in the same place.

(B) Place the stems against the pick; wrap the wire around both the pick and the stems.

(C) Continue wrapping down the pick for 1", then wrap back up the stems, using all the wire.

Wood picks also come without wires. These can be floral-taped to stems or glued to the backs of stem-less items such as pods, charms and novelties.

U-Shaped Floral Pins

Also called "greening pins," these are used to pin moss, ribbon loops, or other items into foam. If the item being secured has a tendency to spring out of the foam, apply a dab of glue to the pin ends before inserting. These can be used as hangers for Styrofoam® and straw wreaths (see page 18).

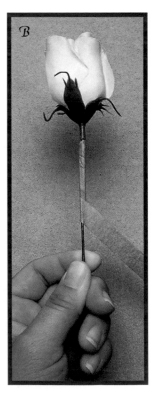

Floral Tape

This is a paper tape which has a waxy coating; stretching the tape as it's being wrapped makes it stick to itself. Use floral tape to secure wire or a pick to a flower stem, lengthening or reinforcing it (also called "stemming a flower").

(A) Place a length of 18-gauge wire next to the stem of a flower.

(B) Wrap the stem and the wire together with floral tape, gently stretching the tape so it adheres to itself. Tape to the end of the wire.

Measuring & Cutting Floral Stems

A "stem" refers to the entire stem of flowers as purchased. When cut apart, the pieces are called "sprigs" or "branches."

When a blossom width is given, measure the open flower head.

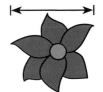

When a blossom height is given, measure only the blossom.

When a stem length is given, measure only the stem.

When a flower length is given, measure from the top of the blossom to the end of the stem.

Unless otherwise specified, flower measurements given within a project include 1½"–2" of stem to be inserted into the design. By cutting the stems with extra length, you are able to adjust the height of the flower within the arrangement, playing with it until it's exactly right. Using tacky craft glue to secure stems lets you, while the glue is still wet, pull out a stem that is too long, trim and reinsert it without destroying the foam. If a stem is too short, lengthen it with a stem wire (see "Floral Tape," page 14), then cut to the correct length.

Wiring a Cone

To wire a cone to attach it to a base:

(A) Use a 10" length of 24-gauge wire. Measure 3" from one end and insert the wire between two rows of cone petals near the bottom.

(B) Wrap the wire around the cone, pulling tightly, then twist the wire ends so they extend from the cone. Use these wire ends to attach the cone to the project. For another look, wrap the wire among the upper petals so the bottom of the cone will show in the project.

Three Ways to Attach a Pick or Stem to a Pod or Cone

(A) Drill a hole into the bottom. Fill the hole with glue and insert the blunt end of an unwired wood pick into the hole.

(B) Wrap the wire of a wood pick around the cone petals, pulling it down inside the cone. Wrap all the wire completely around the cone and then around the pick.

(C) Hot glue a U-shaped floral pin to the cone bottom.

Ribbons & Bows

Some people think one of the most difficult tasks in making a floral project is making the bow. Not so!

The easiest way to learn is to buy a reel of inexpensive acetate ribbon—enough so you don't feel guilty using as much as you want—and practice making bows. The freedom of knowing you can use as much as you want until you get it mastered makes learning much easier than if you use the expensive tapestry ribbon you bought just for a certain project. Eventually, making bows will become second nature (and you'll be asked by everyone in your house, office or neighborhood to please make this one bow for little Jennifer's birthday gift . . .well, you get the picture). Of course, you could offer to teach a class on bow-making to all those friends, family members and neighbors.

We've included instructions, photos and illustrations of the bows used in this book. Generally, if you choose a narrower ribbon than the one suggested, you will need more of it—and to make more loops—to make sure the bow has the same impact within the design. Likewise, if a wider ribbon is chosen, you'll probably want fewer loops to make sure the bow doesn't overpower the project.

Ribbons and bows are beautiful additions to florals, but the styles of ribbons available are almost endless, and it can be confusing to choose just the right pattern for a project. However, you'll find that the flower colors and the style of the arrangement will narrow your choices.

Ribbon Styles

Ribbons are available with different edge treatments; this can be important in design, as some edges will fray with frequent handling. *Woven edge ribbon* has a finished edge which will not fray. This ribbon is easy to use in bows because of its softness and pliability.

Picot ribbon is a woven edge ribbon distinguished by small loops extending outward from each edge. Including picot ribbon with plain ribbons in a multi-ribbon bow adds texture and interest. Picot ribbons add a nice touch to romantic designs.

Wire-edged ribbon is easy to use because it has "memory"; each edge is woven around a thin wire. If a bow becomes crushed it's easy to reshape the loops, making the bow look new. The tails can be rippled and tucked among design components, with the wires holding the shape. The wires can be pulled to easily shirr the ribbon.

Cut edge ribbons are often used in floral work. Less expensive, they are available in many of the same patterns and designs as woven or wire-edged ribbon. To reduce fraying, sizing is added—this stiffens the ribbon, but also means that any creases made in forming the bow will remain visible. Eventually the edges will fray, so handle the ribbon as little as possible.

Paper ribbon has become a floral design staple. Some of these ribbons come twisted into cords and can be used that way, or untwisted to make crinkly flat ribbon. The twisted cords make fun accents twined through and around a bow made from flat paper ribbon. Printed paper ribbons are available both on reels or in packaged lengths. Their patterns are muted, making them nice for dried arrangements. Also available are lacy paper ribbons with cut-out areas resembling eyelet.

Choosing Your Ribbons:

The ribbons you use can determine the entire look of your design. For example, heavy tapestries give a more European look, while narrow satin ribbons add a light, romantic effect. The ribbon should tie the design together and actually become part of it.

In choosing a ribbon, both color and width play important roles. Incompatible colors or textures can produce a jarring effect. Using a ribbon which has all the colors in the design—or nearly all of them—ties the design together.

If one ribbon with the right colors can't be found, use two or three ribbons, each in one of the colors needed, and stack the bows. Make a large bow of the widest ribbon (usually the dominant color in the design), then wire or glue a smaller bow of narrower ribbon to the center of it.

Another method of tying colors together is to make one bow of several different ribbons. Hold them together and handle as if they were one length to make a bow of the desired size and type.

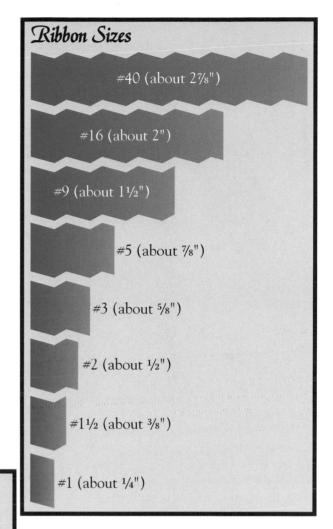

Ribbon Sizes

#40 (about 2⅞")

#16 (about 2")

#9 (about 1½")

#5 (about ⅞")

#3 (about ⅝")

#2 (about ½")

#1½ (about ⅜")

#1 (about ¼")

How Much Do I Need?

Although projects in this book include the yardage needed for each bow in the materials list, you may want to make a different bow. First decide how many loops and tails you want, and how long they will be (if you want a center loop, double its length, add ½" and add this measurement along with the tails.) Then do this easy math:

1. ____" (loop length) x 2 + ½" extra (for the twist) = **A**

2. **A** x (number of loops) = **B**

3. **B** + ____" (tail length) + ____" (tail length) = **C**

4. **C** ÷ 36" = yardage required.

For example:

To make a bow with eight 4" loops, a 6" tail and a 7" tail,

1. 4" x 2" + ½" = **8½"**

2. 8½" x 8 loops = **68"**

3. 68" + 6" (tail length) +7" (tail length) = **81"**

4. 81" ÷ 36" = 2.25 or 2¼ yards.

Many times ribbon is used to bring different design elements together visually. This is done by tucking, rippling or looping ribbon lengths or the bow tails among the other materials in the project. Twisting the ribbon as it's looped adds interest. If the base is visible in one area of the design (such as on a vine wreath with all the flowers at the upper left), wrapping the ribbon around the bare areas will help tie the design together. The ribbon draws your eye into the undecorated space.

Other materials such as cord, braid, pearls, beads or wired star garlands can be used with or in place of ribbon.

For wide ribbons a "couched" effect can be achieved by pinching the ribbon every few inches and wrapping the pinched areas with 30-gauge wire. The ribbon will puff between the wires. Glue the wired areas into the design.

Shoestring Bow

1 Measure the desired tail length from the end of the ribbon, then make a loop of the specified length. Wrap the free end of the ribbon loosely around the center of the bow.

2 Form a loop in the free end of the ribbon and push it through the center loop. Pull the loops in opposite directions to tighten, then pull on the tails to adjust the size of the loops. Trim each tail diagonally or in an inverted V.

Flat Bow

1 Begin with one end of the ribbon and make a center loop the desired length. Twist the ribbon to keep the right side showing.

2 Make a loop the specified length on one side of your thumb. Twist the ribbon and form a matching loop on the other side.

3 Continue making loops of graduating sizes on each side of your thumb, positioning each just under the last loop, until the desired number is reached. For the tails, bring the ribbon end up and hold in place under the bow.

4 Insert a wire length through the center loop. Bring the ends to the back, catching the ribbon end, and twist to secure. Cut the ribbon tails to the desired lengths, then trim each tail diagonally or in an inverted V.

Standup Bow

Measure the desired tail length and hold the ribbon. Make a loop, positioning it to extend upward beside the tail. Repeat to make as many loops as desired. Fold a tail up to match the first tail, then trim the ribbon. Wrap wire tightly around the bottom of the loops to secure.

Ribbon Loops

Beginning at one end of the ribbon, make a loop of the specified size. Fold the tail back to extend beyond the end of the loop; pinch and wire the loop to a wood pick. Trim the tail as desired.

Loopy Bow

1 Measure the desired tail length from the end of the ribbon and make a loop on each side of your thumb. If a center loop is needed, measure the tail length from the end of the ribbon and make the center loop before the bow loops.

2 Continue making loops on each side of your thumb until the desired number is reached (for a ten-loop bow, make five loops on each side).

3 Wrap the center with wire and twist tightly at the back to secure. If a center loop was made, insert the wire through it before twisting the ends at the back. Trim the wire ends. Cut each tail diagonally. Or secure the bow by wrapping a length of ribbon around the center and tying it at the back—this adds a second set of tails.

Loopy Bow with Center Loop

Oblong Bow

1 Form a center loop by wrapping the ribbon around your thumb. Twist the ribbon a half turn to keep the right side showing, then make a loop on one side of the center loop.

2 Make another half twist and another loop on the other side. Make another half twist and form a slightly longer loop on each side of your hand; notice these loops are placed diagonally to the first loops.

3 Make two more twists and loops on the opposite diagonal. Continue for the desired number of loops, making each set slightly longer than the previous set.

4 **For tails:** Bring the ribbon end up and hold in place under the bow. Insert a wire through the center loop, bring the ends to the back of the bow, and twist tightly to secure. Trim each tail diagonally or in an inverted V.

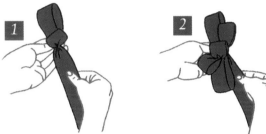

Puffy Bow

1 If a center loop is required, begin with one end of the ribbon length and make the center loop. Twist the ribbon to keep the right side showing. If no center loop is called for, begin with step 2.

2 Make a loop on one side of your thumb. Give the ribbon a twist and make another loop, the same length as the first, on the other side of your thumb. Continue making loops and twists until the desired number is reached (a ten-loop bow has five loops on each side), ending with a twist.

3 **For tails:** Bring the ribbon end up and hold in place under the bow, making a long loop (two or more loops can be made for multiple tails). Insert a wire through the center loop, bring the ends to the back of the bow, and twist tightly to secure. Trim each tail diagonally or in an inverted V.

Collar Bow

1 Form a ribbon length into a circle, crossing the ends in front. Pinch together, forming a bow, and adjust the loop size and tail length. If no tails are desired, form the length into a circle and just barely overlap the ends before pinching into a bow.

2 Wrap the center with wire and twist tightly at the back to secure. Trim the wire ends, then wrap a short length of ribbon over the center wire and glue the ends at the back. Cut each tail diagonally or in an inverted V.

Dior Bow

1 Similar to a collar bow, this one is made with four ribbon lengths. Cut a 3", a 9", an 11", and a 12" length of ribbon. Form the 12" length into a circle.

2 Pinch in the center to make a bow shape.

3 Center the 9" and 11" lengths under the bow for tails and wire them all together at the center. Trim the wire ends, then wrap the 3" length over the wire to cover it and glue the ends at the back. Cut each tail diagonally or in an inverted V.

eucalyptus

echinops

cinnamon
sticks

chili
peppers

cedar

feathers,
pheasant

Frasier fir

German
statice

heather

ammobium

apple slices

artemesia

austral or
rabbit's
foot fern

avena

Identification of Dried Materials

Silk and fresh arrangements can often benefit from the addition of dried and preserved materials. They not only add a new dimension to the design, but can give silk arrangements a more realistic texture. Many of the designs in this book have dried or preserved materials added. The photographs on the following pages isolate the materials used in this book for easy identification. Also use these pages for ideas about making substituions, as covered on page 26. The materials are placed in alphabetical order, beginning at the lower left of each page, and continuing counter-clockwise for easy location.

Because of constant innovation of the commercial preserving industry, dried and preserved flower selections of today are much broader than a few years ago. Flowers and plants can be air-dried, kiln-dried (which helps hold the color), freeze-dried or processed with a dessicant such as silica gel. Glycerin preserving is another popular option because of the soft feel, longevity and color variations. Many flowers which were at one time considered unavailable are now being preserved with great success.

If you want to try your hand at drying flowers, air drying is the easiest method. Remove the lower leaves from the stem and use a soft cloth to dry the flower. Tie several stems together, separating the flower heads as much as possible, and suspend the bunch upside-down in a dry, dark room. Check them periodically; humidity will determine how quickly they dry. Some flowers, such as hydrangea and baby's breath dry best upright, while leaves and moss dry best when lying flat.

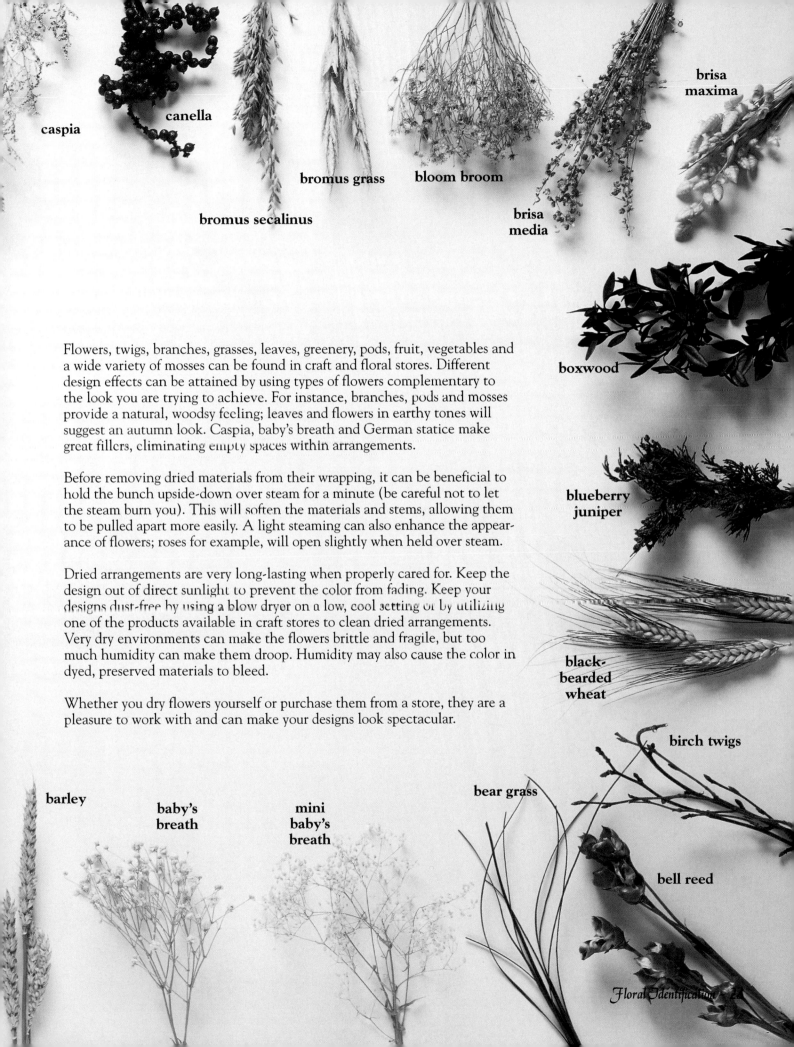

caspia

canella

bromus grass

bromus secalinus

bloom broom

brisa media

brisa maxima

boxwood

blueberry juniper

black-bearded wheat

Flowers, twigs, branches, grasses, leaves, greenery, pods, fruit, vegetables and a wide variety of mosses can be found in craft and floral stores. Different design effects can be attained by using types of flowers complementary to the look you are trying to achieve. For instance, branches, pods and mosses provide a natural, woodsy feeling; leaves and flowers in earthy tones will suggest an autumn look. Caspia, baby's breath and German statice make great fillers, eliminating empty spaces within arrangements.

Before removing dried materials from their wrapping, it can be beneficial to hold the bunch upside-down over steam for a minute (be careful not to let the steam burn you). This will soften the materials and stems, allowing them to be pulled apart more easily. A light steaming can also enhance the appearance of flowers; roses for example, will open slightly when held over steam.

Dried arrangements are very long-lasting when properly cared for. Keep the design out of direct sunlight to prevent the color from fading. Keep your designs dust-free by using a blow dryer on a low, cool setting or by utilizing one of the products available in craft stores to clean dried arrangements. Very dry environments can make the flowers brittle and fragile, but too much humidity can make them droop. Humidity may also cause the color in dyed, preserved materials to bleed.

Whether you dry flowers yourself or purchase them from a store, they are a pleasure to work with and can make your designs look spectacular.

barley

baby's breath

mini baby's breath

bear grass

birch twigs

bell reed

princess pine

poa

plumosus
fern

rice grass

protea

pomegranate

rice flower

silene grass

sponge
mushroom

roses

salal (dried)

sinuata
statice

spruce

Siberian
statice

salal (preserved)

hops

larkspur

leptospurnum

hill flowers

holly

papaver

orange slices

pepper berries

pine cones

phleum

nigella

star flowers

sphagnum moss

reindeer moss

tree fern

mood moss

grey excelsior moss

tı tree

mini holly

stirlingia

ming fern

millet

lichen, forest coral

lilac beauty achillia

lotus pod

lichen, black

Floral Identification - 27

Substitution of Materials

We make every effort to use widely distributed floral materials in our designs. But, with more than 100,000 new items introduced every year, it can sometimes be difficult to find all the exact materials required for any one project. With a little creativity, it's an easy task to substitute other flowers for ones listed.

When substituting, find flowers that are similar to those listed in the project. Check to make sure each is approximately the size required with as many blossoms as needed. If you're substituting a different type of flower, make sure it's the same shape: A 3" wide rose or carnation might be substituted for a 3" wide mum. The texture will be a little different, but the design shouldn't suffer for it.

Sometimes it may be difficult to find just the exact Christmas pick described in the text of a project. In this case, the colors and "look" of the pick used become more important than exactly what is in it. If the project is to be woodsy or have a natural look, then the pick needs to have that same look in the desired colors.

Substituting dried materials when the correct type can't be found is also easy. If you're looking for a certain cone or pod, any cone or pod of similar size and color could replace the original. If several styles of pods are needed to complete a project, it's probably important that different pods are used, but maybe not those exact ones. (If the same pod is used throughout, the design might become boring; different styles of pods add texture and interest to a piece.)

If a certain dried flower or grass in unavailable, look at that material in the photo and try to find one which is similar. For instance, fillers such as gypsophila, rice grass, baby's breath and caspia can easily substitute for each other because they have similar characteristics, with fine flowers or seeds which will extend equally well among the larger components of the arrangement. If the product is bulky or heavy, substitute a product of similar weight.

Many times silk flowers can replace dried ones in an arrangement, too. Silk baby's breath comes in different colors and is easy to add into an arrangement which originally calls for dried baby's breath. There are many latex fruits, pods and vegetables which are great substitutes for similar dried materials. The advantage to using silk and latex pieces in place of dried materials is their longevity. They don't shatter like dried flowers, allowing the arrangement to remain beautiful longer.

It's a little more difficult to substitute dried flowers for silk. Generally, air-dried blossoms are smaller, thus harder to use as a large focal point in a design. Not every polysilk is available as a dried flower, so substituting other flower types may be necessary when converting a silk arrangement to drieds.

If colors need to be changed to match your decor, determine the dominant color in the design and choose the number of flowers listed in the desired color. Repeat through the list, substituting your chosen colors for the ones listed. When you've gathered all the flowers, hold them together in a bunch to make sure the new colors blend well. If there's a ribbon in the design, hold it with the flowers to be sure everything coordinates. Substituting can be an exciting adventure in creativity! Be patient and play with the colors, sizes and textures to make sure they will blend well and produce the look and feeling desired.

Working with Vinyl Wreaths, Garlands and Picks

Fluff and shape the individual sprigs of a piece to achieve a natural look before using. Pull the sprigs away from the main stem of a garland, angling them in the same direction. If the garland is to be displayed on a flat surface, pull all the exposed sprigs flat on the under side. Shape the sprigs to angle naturally. Wreaths are usually shaped with the sprigs angled in the same direction, clockwise or counterclockwise, for the most natural look. Pull the sprigs forward for a fuller look. Shape the sprigs of individual greeenery stems to resemble a tree branch. As with most greens, the branches can be shaped flatter or rounded, depending on the desired look.

Storing your Christmas Decorations

With the exception of the designs in the fresh greens section, the floral arrangements in this book can be used and enjoyed for many Christmas seasons if they are stored properly the rest of the year. Most items should be boxed individually in sturdy cardboard containers. Wreath boxes can be purchased during the holiday season at most shipping supply stores. Ornament boxes with individual sections inside are ideal for storing floral ornaments. Garlands should be carefully and loosely coiled in flat boxes. Tissue can be packed around an item to keep it stable in the box; foam chips or heaver paper can crush the florals, especially drieds. Be sure the item is clean before packing it away. Light dust can be removed with a blow dryer on the low-cool setting or a spray product especially formulated to clean silk or dried florals is available at craft stores.

Coloring or Spraying Floral Materials

Paint is the simplest method of coloring floral materials. There are spray paints made especially for this purpose, which have the properties of tints. Use of traditional spray paints on florals can make them flat or dull. The floral paints come in a wide variety of colors. When using floral paints, begin with a very light misting of paint, holding the material 8"–12" away from the nozzle. Let dry; repeat until the desired coverage is attained. Spraying several light coats of a color onto a flower produces a more natural look than one heavy coating. Spray glitters are also available and can add vibrance to a holiday design. Glitters can be used alone for subtle effects or in combination with the metallic spray paints for a dazzling look.

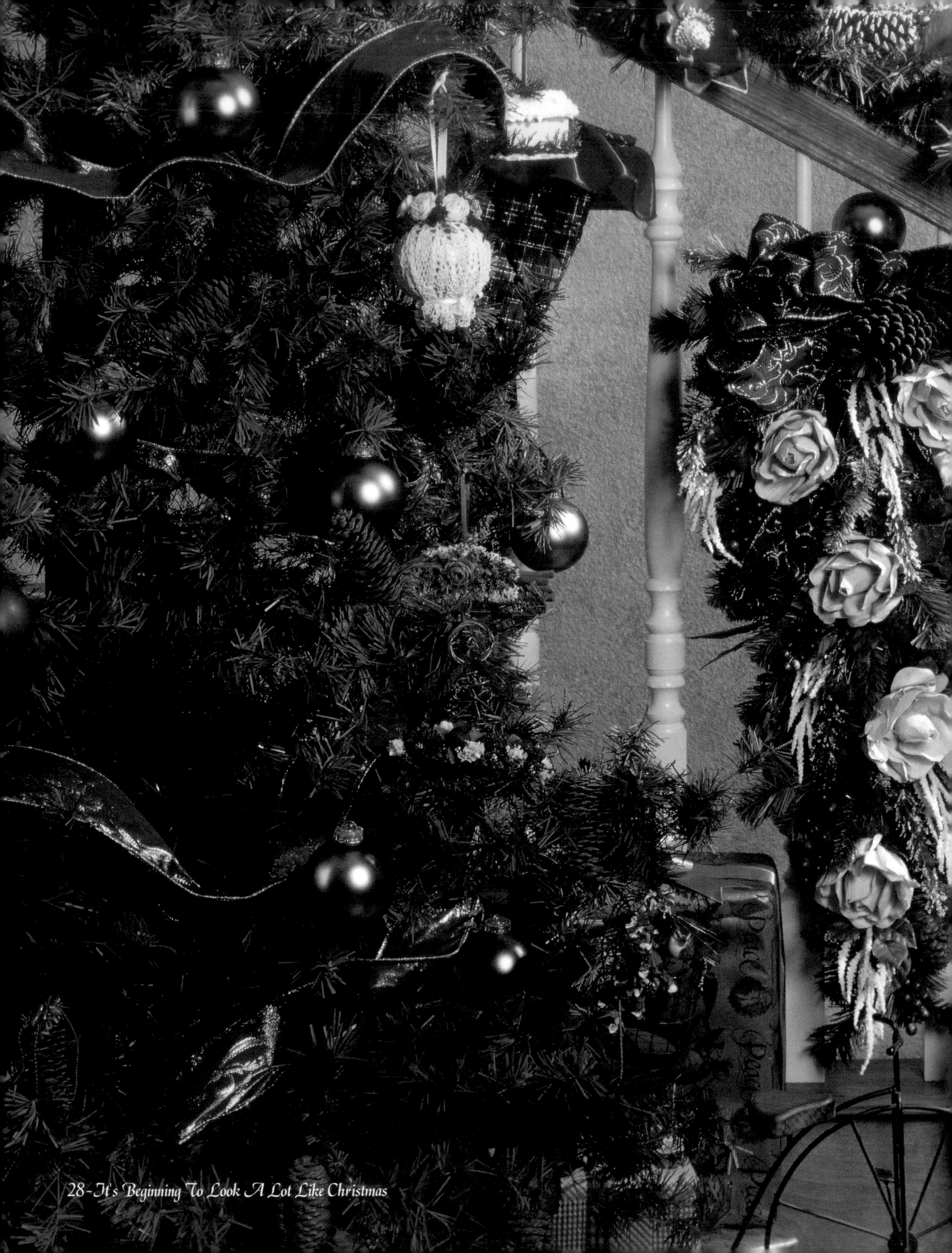

It's Beginning to Look a Lot Like Christmas

In anticipation of loved ones gathering together for Christmas, we decorate our homes with traditional symbols of the season. We deck the trees with treasured ornaments, surround them with gaily wrapped gifts and hang wreaths on our doors to convey a cheery welcome to all who enter.

The following pages contain some tips and guidelines for decorating the tree and are designed to take the mystery out of achieving a balanced look. Also included are photographs of ideas for using the designs featured in this book to decorate different rooms of the house.

Wreaths, garlands, swags and centerpieces adorn an entry alcove, an office, the dining area and a kitchen, all providing Christmas cheer and charm. Also featured are a southwest living room setting along with a girl's and a boy's room, contributing creative ideas to decorating schemes.

This section is filled with wonderful settings which feature the projects from the book and methods for using them to enhance the Christmas feeling through placement within rooms. These pieces were created especially to bring the warmth and festive feeling throughout the home.

Tips for a Well Decorated Tree

Lights

Attach the lights to the tree before adding any ornaments; keep the lights lit so you can check the effect as you work. Start at the top of the tree, winding downward in a zig-zag pattern. Weave the lights back and forth through the branches to give the tree depth and to hide the cord. Even if the tree is placed in a corner, be sure to string lights all the way around at the top, as most of the top of the tree is visible from different angles. Choose colors and styles which complement your other decorations. The more lights you use, the more brilliant your tree will be.

Lighting needs

Tree Height	# of Mini Lights
2 feet	35–50
3 feet	70–100
4 feet	100–140
6 feet	200–280
7 feet	315–450
8 feet	400–650
9 feet	600–900
10 feet	800–1100

Garlands

Draping garlands creates a symmetrical framework to highlight your tree and ornaments. Start at the bottom back of the tree and wire or wrap one end of the garland around a branch tip. Drape it around the base and over the lower branches so that it hangs evenly and freely; move branch tips if necessary. If there is no branch tip where the garland should hang, wrap wire around it and hang it from a higher branch. Repeat for the succeeding rows, spacing them evenly. Trim the branch tips between the rows if necessary so they appear even. To join garlands, wire the ends together at the back of the tree. See the draping examples at the right.

For added elegance, tie shoestring bows (see page 141) of ribbon or raffia to branch tips under the garlands, spacing them evenly. Ribbon or raffia strands also can be loosely wrapped around the garlands to match the bows.

Garland needs

Tree Height	Garland Length
2 feet	15'–20'
4 feet	30'–40'
6 feet	50'–75'
7 feet	75'–95'
9 feet	125'–150'

Ornaments

For the best results, follow the color and design scheme set up by your lights and garlands. Place satin balls on inside branches, then add glass balls to both the inside and tips of the branches. Fill dark or empty spaces with glass balls or attach them to hang from under a garland. Wire three different solid-color balls together before hanging for a special touch. Attach the large ornaments first, evenly spaced, then smaller items such as icicles and candy canes on the outer branches.

Special Touches for the Tree

Leftover items from your craft drawer combined with glue, a little time and some imagination can yield fantastic results. For some non-traditional decor for your tree, try these ideas:

Roll a paper doily into a cone shape, staple or glue together and stuff with silk or dried flowers. Use ribbon to make a shoestring bow and a hanging loop.

To add a full look to a sparsely branched tree, add clusters of baby's breath, birch branches or other dried materials tucked loosely between the branches. These materials can also be used vertically at the top of the tree to create height.

Tuck silk flowers or bushes in complementary colors among the tree branches to add color and fullness. Pushing stems deeper into the tree will create more depth.

To create the illusion of a fuller tree, push crumpled tulle deep into the branches. Ivory or gold tulle will add elegance, while pink, lavender or rose tulle will enhance a Victorian tree.

More creative ideas:
- Glue mushroom birds into straw nests and wire to the tree.
- Make large ribbon bows with long streamers. Position them at the top of the tree and let the tails drape vertically over the tree to the floor. Dramatic effects can be created by varying the lengths or looping the tails among the branches.
- Tie many bows of coordinating colors and wire them to the ends of tree branches, creating continuity among all the decorations.
- Cut inexpensive printed holiday fabric into strips and weave them as a garland among the tree branches.
- Glue clusters of small pine cones and dried roses onto pieces of dried bark about the size of a leaf. Tuck them among the branches or attach a ribbon hanger and hang them.

Entry Alcove

The wide variety of projects in this book fit into any home. To begin, choose small areas in which to concentrate your decorating. This setting is a perfect example of how to decorate a small entry or living room space. The Burgundy Rose Wreath (page 61) on the wall works well with the colors in the the Magnolia Garland (page 82) on the banister. The Potpourri Birdfeeder (page 74) on the table completes this holiday nook.

Office Library

The pieces shown here are perfect for an office, lending a refined natural feeling to the room. Lotus pods which have been sprayed metallic gold replace flowers in the Burnished Gold Festoon (page 87) draped over the fireplace. The colors of the Potpourri Vase (page 139) on the reading table complement the colors of Reva's Wreath (page 60), which uses pine cones instead of the more traditional evergreens.

Dining Area

An endless variety of looks can be achieved with the vast choices of projects included in this book. This elegant setting is a great example of well-matched designs; they complement each other in both style and color. The Banquet Garland (page 83) gives a casual buffet sophisticated elegance. The French Horn Wreath (page 54) fits in well with this setting without

using the same materials or even colors . . . a great example of how to mix and match. The Place Card Holders (page 136) subtly bring the two looks and colors together, providing a harmonious setting.

Kitchen

Although the Poinsettia Window Valance (page 91) is designed to hang over a window, it is displayed here over the valance which provides a nice backdrop for the twigs. The Blue Tartan Wreath (page 51) is a nice touch on any wall or nook, but hanging it on a window will liven up a winter day. The Folk Santa Candleholder (page 73) is designed to sit on any flat surface. Replacing a kitchen or living room decoration with a seasonal arrangement, such as the Folk Santa Candleholder, will provide Christmas cheer during the holidays. And you will be surprised how much you enjoy the "old" piece once it returns after the holidays!

Southwest Living Room

Many people just think of Christmas as red poinsettias and green holly, but here is an interesting and clever twist. This Southwestern room is accented by the Southwest Christmas arrangement (page 64) on the table, along with the Triple Wheat Swag (page 88) and Garland with Naturals (page 85) on the wall behind it. These are three non-traditional Christmas designs that work well in decor styles which are not easily changed for the holidays.

Den

Little touches of holiday cheer can be added to any room. A bookish den doesn't need flowery designs; it thrives with quieter country designs such as this Basket Trio Centerpiece (page 72) on the table and the Pine Cone Pendulum (page 52) on the wall. Both feature pheasant feathers, lending a masculine appeal to this corner during the holidays.

Dining Room

Though the holiday season involves many parties, be sure to bring the season into your more private moments. The Terra Cotta Trio (page 75) makes a striking centerpiece with its lit candles while bringing out the colors in the Terra Cotta Garland (page 80) on the wall.

Bedroom

You may not consider decorating your bedroom for Christmas, but doing so can add some of the most personal and meaningful touches to your home. The Country Swag (page 89) on the wall blends well with the rest of the room, and the Prairie Pine Tree (page 65) on bedside table emphasizes the Christmas feel brought to the room.

Living Room

While a bit non-traditional, these two arrangements feature large white magnolias which are perfect for a Southern or a formal home. The Southern Elegance Wreath (page 40) blends well with the Speedy Magnolia Swag (page 137) on the table and the gilded candle sticks, mirror and picture frame all coordinate to complete the elegant feeling of this room.

Fireplace Mantle

For a less formal home, try pieces with folk figures such as the Santa's Forest (page 42). The Christmas Card Holder (page 95) on the wall is another casual and warm piece; it works very well with the Dried Rose Arrangement (page 70) on the mantle beside it to create this cozy, country corner.

Girl's Room

Though the kids love the holidays, you may not think of decorating their rooms for Christmas. Try placing some very simple or easy arrangements in their rooms, such as a small tree decorated with some of the ornaments from the Treasured Trims sections. For a final touch, add a larger arrangement that fits the room's decor such as the Angel Bunny Wreath (page 49) or the Romantic Garland (page 79).

Boy's Room

Decorate a young boy's room by choosing to create the pieces in this book with similar items, such as the Teddy Bear Garland (page 81) on the wall and the Teddy Bear Sleigh (page 68) on the dresser. Add the Holiday Chair (page 67) on the table to reinforce the color scheme and add a bit of charm and whimsy to the setting.

Rich & Radiant Wreaths

Whether you adorn every corner of your home for the holidays or choose to decorate more simply, you will probably incorporate a wreath into your Christmas decor. Wreaths are the most popular element in traditional decorating schemes, especially for Christmas. In days of old, wreaths of evergreen branches were hung on the door of a home during late winter to remind the inhabitants that fair weather and green pastures were just around the corner.

There is a wide variety of wreath bases available today, making endless design possibilities! Greenery and grapevine wreaths can be totally covered or embellished with a simple crescent design. Pinecone wreaths make a statement without many additional components and look wonderful when highlighted with a partial design or just lightly accented.

If a certain base is unavailable but you love the design, replace the wreath base with a similar type. Make sure it is compatible with the type of materials used. And, because the wreath will be viewed from all angles, be careful to bring the materials over the outer edges and avoid bare areas.

Christmas wreaths can be whimsical like the Angel Bunny Wreath on page 49, woodsy, as with Santa's Forest on page 42, or elegant, such as the Iced Eucalyptus wreath on page 57. The unusual color scheme of the Golden Star Wreath on page 58 produces gorgeous results; the wreath is brimming with rich tones and textures, as well as graceful lines.

Many wreath styles have been created for this section. We're sure you'll find several to make for your home and as gifts for very special friends.

Southern Elegance Wreath

24" green vinyl pine wreath
2¾ yards of 2½" wide gold satin tapestry
  ribbon with wired edges
1 yard of ¼" wide white fused pearls
2 stems of white latex magnolias, each
  with one 6" wide and one 5" wide
  blossom, 1 bud, 2 clusters of many ½"
  wide grapes and twelve 4"–7" long
  leaves
2 stems of white latex cotton, each with 3
  branches of one or two 2" wide cotton
  bolls
1 stem of gold latex bridal wreath with 9
  sprigs of three 1" wide blossom clusters
2 oz. of 7"–9" long dried birch twigs
3 oz. of white dried German statice
metallic gold spray paint
newspapers
12" of 24-gauge wire
low temperature glue gun and sticks

1   Lay the birch twigs on newspapers; spray them with gold paint and let dry. Cut each magnolia stem to 16". Wire the stem to the left side of the wreath angling downward with the larger blossom at 7:00. Wire the other magnolia stem curving upward with the larger blossom at 9:00.

2   Cut the cotton into six 8" sprigs. Glue one sprig beside each magnolia blossom as shown. Glue one sprig to extend from behind each magnolia bud. Use the ribbon to make an oblong bow (see page 20) with a center loop, four 5" loops and two 26" tails. Glue the bow between the large magnolias; arrange one tail upward and one downward, tucking them between the magnolia blossoms as shown.

3   Cut the bridal wreath stem into nine 4" sprigs, each with three blossom clusters. Glue them evenly spaced among the magnolias and cotton sprigs. Cut the gold birch twigs to 7"–9" and glue evenly spaced among the florals, extending outward and forward.

4   Cut the German statice into 5" sprigs and glue evenly spaced among the magnolia stems. Cut the pearl string into six 6" lengths. Form a loop with each length and wire the ends to secure. Glue the pearl loops near the magnolia blossoms as shown. Attach a wire loop hanger (see page 12) at the top back of the wreath.

Romantic Poinsettia Wreath

20" green vinyl pine wreath

4⅔ yards of 1½" wide pink/bur-
gundy/green/navy poinsettia print
ribbon with gold wired edges

1 pink silk poinsettia bush with five
6" wide blossoms

1 stem of green silk rose leaves with
nine 5" sprigs of three 2"–3"
leaves

2 stems of gold plastic coral, each
with three 7" long sprigs of many
4"–5" branches

4 oz. of burgundy preserved salal

4 oz. of white dried caspia

3 oz. of pink preserved leptospurnum

3 oz. of blue dried echinops

eight 3"–4" long pine cones, painted red then flocked white

12" of 24-gauge wire

low temperature glue gun and sticks

1 Use the ribbon to make an oblong bow (see
page 20) with a center loop, two 3" loops, six
3½" loops, two 4½" loops and two 8" tails. Glue
the bow to the center bottom of the wreath.
Weave the remaining ribbon into the greenery
around the wreath as shown; glue in several places
to secure. Cut the poinsettias into five 4" sprigs
and glue evenly spaced around the wreath.

2 Cut the rose leaf stem into nine 5" sprigs with
three leaves each; glue evenly spaced among
the greenery on the front inner and outer edges.
Cut the salal into 5" sprigs and glue as for the rose
leaves.

3 Cut the leptospurnum into 4"–7" sprigs and
glue among the florals. Glue a pine cone under
and on each side of the bow. Glue the remaining
pine cones evenly spaced around the wreath as
shown.

4 Cut the echinops into 4" sprigs and glue them
in groups of three around each poinsettia in a
triangular pattern. Cut the coral into twelve 4"–5"
sprigs and the caspia into 3"–5" sprigs; glue them
evenly spaced around the wreath. Attach a wire
hanger (see page 12) to the upper back of the
wreath.

Santa's Forest

16" green eucalyptus wreath
1¼ yards of 2⅝" wide
    green/red/purple/brown/
    black printed ribbon
2 red latex raspberry picks, each
    with five ½" wide raspberries
1 stem of purple silk violets with
    ten 1" wide blossoms
3 oz. of white preserved ti-tree
eleven 2" long pine cones
one 9" tall Santa figure with a
    cardboard tube body, red/green
    velvet cloak, burlap bag with
    three ½" wide pine cones, a
    purple forget-me-not sprig and a
    cluster of many ¼" plastic
    berries with plastic greens
7" of ⅜" wide wooden dowel
12" of 24-gauge wire
low temperature glue gun and
    sticks

1 Spread glue on one end of the dowel and insert into Santa's body tube and let dry. Glue the other end of the dowel into the bottom of the wreath, so the Santa figure is centered in the wreath opening as shown. Attach a wire hanger (see page 12) to the top back of the wreath.

2 Cut four 4½" lengths of ribbon. Pinch one end of one length and wrap with wire to secure; repeat with the other three lengths. Use the remaining ribbon to make an oblong bow (see page 20) with a center loop, two 2½" loops and two 5" tails. Cut an inverted "V" in the end of each ribbon and each bow tail. Glue the bow to the center bottom of the wreath. Glue the wired ribbon lengths around the wreath, as shown.

3 Glue the pine cones evenly spaced among the eucalyptus and around the bow. Cut the ti-tree into 4"–6" sprigs and glue them evenly spaced around the wreath as shown.

4 Cut the violets into ten 3" sprigs and glue evenly spaced among the eucalyptus.
Cut each raspberry pick into two 3" sprigs, one with two berries and one with three. Glue them evenly spaced on each side of and under Santa as shown in the large photo.

13" grapevine wreath
1⅔ yards of ¼" wide
  green/red/gold twisted
  cord
2¾ yards of 2⅝" wide
  red/green/gold plaid ribbon
1 green vinyl pine pick with
  twenty-four 6" long
  sprigs
1 green silk holly bush with
  thirteen 3" long sprigs of
  six 2"–3" long leaves and
  one 1" wide cluster of
  ¼" wide red berries
1 stem of red latex buds with
  twelve 7" long sprays of
  many ⅛" wide buds
three 5" tall painted tin
  Santa ornaments, each
  with jointed legs, holding
  a star overhead
three 3" wide red ball candles
12" of 24-gauge wire
low temperature glue gun
  and sticks

Santa's Lantern

1 Cut the plaid ribbon into three 33" lengths and make three oblong bows (see page 20) each with a center loop, two 3½" loops and two 7" tails. Glue the bows equally spaced around to the outside of the wreath as shown. Cut the cord into three 20" lengths. Tie one length to the wreath over each bow and knot the ends to form the lantern hanger.

2 Glue the candles to the wreath between the cords. Cut the pine into twenty-four 6" sprigs, divide in half. Glue two sprigs to the wreath above each bow, angled to the inside in opposite directions. At the end of these sprigs, glue two more pine sprigs so the ends cover the base of the candles as shown. Repeat around the entire wreath top, using 12 sprigs. Turn the wreath over and repeat on the bottom, using the remaining sprigs.

3 Cut the holly into thirteen 3" sprigs; glue one to the right and left of each bow around the outside of the wreath. Glue another sprig of holly above each bow. Glue the remaining four sprigs evenly spaced among the pine on the bottom of the wreath.

4 Wire one Santa figure under each bow. Cut the bud spray into twelve 7" sprays and evenly glue them flat among the pine branches on the top and underside of the wreath.

Cinnamon & Apple Roses

20" green vinyl pine wreath with six 2" long pine cones

2⅔ yards of 2⅝" wide black/red/green/gold partridge in a pear tree print fabric ribbon

3 latex apple picks, each with one 1½" wide apple, one 1" wide orange/burgundy raspberry, three ½" wide orange/burgundy berries, four ⅜" wide burgundy berries and eight 2"–2½" long leaves

1 stem of yellow latex raspberries with four 6" sprigs of two to three ½" wide berries and three to five 2½"–3½" long leaves

nine 5½"–7" long cinnamon sticks

sixteen 1"–2" long pine cones

25 dried apple slices, each 2" long

4 oz. of dried birch or buck twigs

3 oz. of dried avena

12" of 24-gauge wire

low temperature glue gun and sticks

1   Use the ribbon to make a puffy bow (see page 20) with a center loop, six 5" loops and two 15" tails. Glue it at 11:00 with one tail at 3:00 and the other at 5:00. Glue the picks at 1:00, 3:00 and 8:00, angled as shown.

2   Wire the cinnamon sticks together in groups of three, spreading the sticks as shown. Glue them to the wreath at 2:00, 5:00 and 9:00. Use five apple slices to make a rose: wrap the first slice in a tight roll, then wrap the other four flaring around it as shown. Wire the slices together at the base of the rose to secure. Repeat to make four more roses; glue them evenly spaced around the wreath.

3   Cut the berries into four 5" sprigs; cut one of these sprigs in half. Glue all the sprigs evenly spaced among the pine as shown. Glue the pine cones around the wreath among the greenery.

4   Cut the avena into 3"–4" sprigs and glue them evenly among the greenery. Glue the birch twigs evenly to the outside edges of the wreath. Let the glue dry and then glue the other end to the inside edge of the wreath to make a light "cage" over the wreath as shown in the large photo. Make a wire hanger (see page 12) at the top back of the wreath.

Christmas from the Garden

16" wide root wreath
1 green vinyl pine pick with six 6" branches, each with three 5" sprigs
1¾ yards of 2½" wide tan/burgundy check
  ribbon
forty 26" long raffia strands
1 stem of green latex holly with four 5" long
  sprigs of four or five 2"–3" long leaves
  and a cluster of ½" wide red berries
1 stem of green latex holly with four 2"–3"
  long leaves (no berries)
1 oz. of dried sphagnum moss
four 5"–6" long garden tools; hoe, rake,
  fork, shovel
five 2¼" wide terra cotta pots
12" of 24-gauge wire
low temperature glue gun and sticks

1 Cut the pine into six 6" branches. Glue two to the bottom center of the wreath, facing left and right. Repeat at the top center, then glue another branch under each upper branch, extending half way down each side of the wreath.

2 Divide the raffia in half and use each half to make a collar bow (see page 21) with two 3½" loops and 6" tails. Cut two 30" lengths of plaid ribbon and use each to make a collar bow with two 4" loops and two 6" tails. Cut the remaining plaid ribbon lengthwise into two 1¼" wide pieces. Cut 2" off one piece and set aside for step 4. Wrap one length around each side of the wreath, gluing the ends at the back to secure. Glue a raffia bow to the center of a plaid bow. Reverse to glue the plaid bow over the raffia bow. Glue them to the wreath as shown.

3 Glue a pot under the upper bow, with the rim facing downward. Glue one pot at each end of the pine sprigs as shown. Pull the moss apart into five 1" tufts and glue a tuft into each pot.

4 Cut the holly leaves from the stem that has just leaves. Glue two leaves to the center of the top bow, one facing left and one right. Glue the other two leaves above the lower bow loops, facing upward. Cut the berried holly into four 5" sprigs. Glue the four sprigs with berries evenly spaced around the wreath as shown in the large photo. Cut a 5" length of raffia from a bow tail and use it to tie two tools together. Wrap the other remaining tools with the 2" ribbon piece from step 2. Glue the tools to the bow centers. Attach a wire hanger (see page 12) at the top back of the wreath.

Fisherman's Holiday

20" green vinyl pine gar-
land with fifteen 2½"–3"
pine cones
3 ¼ yards of 3" wide tan
open-weave wired jute
ribbon
1 stem of red/green latex
raspberries with four 6"
long sprigs of two to three
½"–1" wide berries and
many 2"–3" long leaves
3 oz. of blue preserved holly
2 oz. of dried nigella
six 4" long blue/red/yellow
wooden fish ornaments
eight 1 ½" long corks
12" of 24-gauge wire
low temperature glue gun
and sticks

1 Use the ribbon to make a puffy bow (see page 20) with a center loop, four 4½" loops and one 68" tail. Glue it to the center top of the wreath, then arrange the tail around the wreath as shown. Glue to secure. Pull on the tail and loops from the sides to open the mesh.

2 Glue one fish ornament at 9:00, toward the outside of the wreath and one at 10:00 toward the inside. Glue two fish at 6:00 and two at 3:00 as shown.

3 Cut the raspberries into four 6" sprigs and glue evenly spaced around the wreath. Cut the holly into 4" long two-leaf sprigs and glue evenly spaced among the greenery.

4 Cut the nigella into 4" sprigs and glue them in groups of two or three evenly spaced around the wreath, alternating from inside to outside as shown. Glue the corks evenly spaced around the wreath. Make a wire hanger (see page 12) at the upper back of the wreath.

Winter Wilderness Wreath

18" grapevine wreath
2 stems of burgundy latex poinsettias, each
  with one 9" wide blossom
1 stem of green latex leaves with thirteen
  4"–6" long leaves
2 stems of purple latex grapes, each with one
  7" long cluster of many ¾" wide grapes
2 stems of purple latex mini grapes, each
  with three 4" long clusters of many ½"
  wide grapes
3 oz. of burgundy preserved eucalyptus
3 oz. of burgundy preserved mini holly
3 oz. of green preserved ming fern
2 oz. of dried brisa media
12" of 24-gauge wire
low temperature glue gun and sticks

1   Holding the wreath tightly, remove
    the bindings. Gently pull on the
vines to loosen them. Cut fifteen 30"
vines from the back of the wreath to use
in step 4. Wrap wire around the remaining wreath at 3:00 and 9:00. Cut the
poinsettia stems to 3" and glue one to the
wreath at 5:00 and one at 7:00, angled
slightly upward. Cut the latex leaves off
the stem and glue them evenly spaced
around the wreath from 5:00 to 11:00.
Cut the eucalyptus into 8" sprigs and glue
them in clusters of three in a counter-
clockwise direction as shown leaving the
area between 1:00 and 11:00 open.

2   Glue one grape cluster at 10:00 and
    one at 5:00, both angled downward.
Glue one of the mini grape stems at 6:00
angled downward. Cut the other mini
grape stem into one 5" and one 8" sprig. Glue the 5" sprig at
3:00 and the 8" sprig at 1:00.

3   Cut the mini holly into 9" sprigs; moving clockwise, glue
    them evenly spaced around the wreath from 1:00 to
11:00 as shown. Cut the ming fern into 7" sprigs and repeat.

4   Cut the brisia media into 6" sprigs and glue evenly spaced
    around the wreath from 1:00 to 10:00. Glue one end of a
twig from step 1 into the outer area on the wreath. When dry,
bring the end across the wreath front, tuck among the vines
and glue. Continue, inserting the twigs evenly around the
wreath, overlapping the twigs when possible. Attach a wire
hanger (see page 12) at the top back of the wreath.

Birch Crescent

11" birch bark wreath

1 ¾ yards of 3" wide burgundy twist paper ribbon

1 stem of burgundy fabric dogwood with an 18" long section of five 2½" wide blossoms, ½" wide buds and many 2" long leaves

1 stem of red latex berries with seven 4" long sprigs of five ½" wide berries

4 oz. of green preserved cedar

2 oz. of white preserved rice flower

2 oz. of white preserved ti-tree

seven 1½" long pine cones

12" of 24-gauge wire

low temperature glue gun and stick

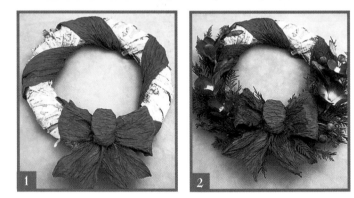

1 Cut a 24" length of ribbon and make an oblong bow (see page 20) with a center loop, two 3" loops and two 4" tails. Glue one end of the remaining ribbon at the bottom of the wreath; wrap the ribbon three times around the wreath as shown and glue the end to secure. Glue the bow to the bottom front.

2 Cut the cedar into 4" sprigs and glue in a crescent extending upward from the center bottom to 2:00 and 10:00. Glue more sprigs among the bows loops. Cut the dogwood into two 9" sprigs one with two blossoms and the other with three blossoms. Glue to the wreath as shown.

3 Cut the berries into seven 4" sprigs and glue evenly spaced among the florals. Cut the rice flower into 2" sprigs and glue as for the berries, with 4–6 sprigs among the bow loops.

4 Cut the ti tree into 3"–5" sprigs and glue them among the other materials as for the rice flower sprigs. Glue the pine cones evenly spaced among the other materials, alternating the angles as shown in the large photo. Attach a wire hanger (see page 12) at the top back of the wreath.

Angel Bunny Wreath

14"x16" oval vine wreath with
   woven vine backing
one 9" tall cream muslin bunny
   angel
2⅔ yards of 2½" wide
   ivory/white/gold sheer checked
   ribbon with gold wired edges
2 stems of pearlized ivory latex
   grapes, each with three 3"–4" long
   clusters of many ⅜"–½" wide
   grapes
2 stems of white silk roses, each
   with three 2" wide blossoms, two
   ½" wide buds and many 1½"
   long leaves
6 oz. of green preserved cedar
2 oz. of red dried pepper berries
six 1½" long pine cones
2 oz. of silver-glitter preserved
   Australian fern
12" of 24-gauge wire
low temperature glue gun and sticks

1 Cut the cedar into 6"–8" sprigs and glue them
   extending up from the wreath center bottom
in a crescent shape as shown. Glue the bunny at
the center bottom of the wreath, sitting on the
cedar and leaning against the vine backing.

2 Cut the rose stems to 9" and glue them to the
   wreath with the stems at the center bottom,
following the curves of the wreath. Cut the grapes
into six 4" sprigs and glue three evenly spaced
among the cedar on each side of the bunny, angled
as shown.

3 Cut the pepper berries into 2" sprigs and glue
   them evenly spaced among the cedar. Glue
three pine cones on each side of the bunny, evenly
spaced among the cedar.

4 Cut the fern into 5" sprigs and glue among the
   cedar, extending up and outward. Use the ribbon to make an oblong bow (see page 20) with a
center loop, two 3" loops, two 4" loops, two 7" loops
and two 15" tails. Glue the bow to the upper right of
the wreath as shown. Crinkle the tails and glue
them down the sides of the wreath. Attach a wire
hanger (see page 12) at the top back of the wreath.

Santa & His Reindeer

20" green vinyl pine wreath

3 ¼ yards of 3 ½" wide red/green/white/blue Christmas print ribbon with gold wired edges

1 green vinyl pine pick with twenty 5" long flocked sprigs

1 stem of blue latex berries with fifteen 1" wide clusters of many berries

1 stem of white flocked latex twigs with nine 6" long branches

three 5 ½" tall crackle-painted tin Santa figures

three 4" tall white reindeer jingle bells

12" of 24-gauge wire

low temperature glue gun and sticks

1 Use the ribbon to make an oblong bow (see page 20) with a center loop, two 4" loops, two 5½" loops and one 68" tail. Glue the bow to the center top of the wreath. Loop and tuck the tail around the wreath front, gluing it into the pine sprigs every 3"–4".

2 Glue the Santa figures and reindeer evenly spaced around the wreath front, angled as shown.

3 Cut the pine pick into twenty 5" sprigs and glue them evenly among the pine branches of the wreath, angled alternately toward the inside and outside of the wreath.

4 Cut the berries into five 5" sprigs with two clusters each and five 2" sprigs with one cluster each. Glue them evenly spaced around the wreath, alternating as shown. Cut the white twigs into nine 6" sprigs and glue them clockwise around the wreath, spacing them as shown in the large photo. Attach a wire hanger (see page 12) at the top back of the wreath.

German Statice Wreath

16" white German statice wreath

1½ yards of 2½" wide red/white/green plaid ribbon with wired edges

3 iced latex poinsettia picks, each with a 5½" wide white poinsettia blossom, a 1½" wide gold pomegranate, 1 cluster of seven ½" wide white berries and two to three 3"–4" wide leaves

three 4" long stems of red latex frosted grapes, each with three 3" clusters of many ½" wide grapes

thirteen 1½" wide pine cone roses

3 oz. of dried black-bearded wheat

2 oz. of red preserved tree fern

12" of 24-gauge wire

low temperature glue gun and sticks

1 Cut the poinsettia picks to 8" and glue them to the wreath at 3:00, 9:00 and 12:00. Shape and spread the leaves out to the sides of the picks.

2 Use the ribbon to make a puffy bow (see page 20) with a center loop, four 4" loops and two 7" tails. Glue it to the center bottom of the wreath. Cut the grapes into nine 4" sprigs; and glue one sprig below the bow and the rest evenly among the poinsettia picks.

3 Cut the wheat into 5" sprigs; glue them to extend counterclockwise among the poinsettias and around the bow. Glue one pine cone rose below the bow and the rest evenly spaced among the florals.

4 Cut the tree fern into 5"–7" sprigs. Glue three under the bow and the rest among the other materials, angled counterclockwise as shown. Attach a wire hanger (see page 12) at the top back of the wreath.

Pine Cone Pendulum

14" wide pine cone wreath
2 yards of 2½" wide red/green/white plaid rib-
    bon with red wired edges
1 red silk poinsettia stem with a 7" wide blossom
1 stem of red latex berries with two 3" long and
    two 5" long sprigs of many ¼"–½" wide
    berries and ten to twelve 2¼" long leaves
2 stems of red latex raspberries, each with two
    2" clusters of five ½" wide berries and three
    to five 2" long leaves
1 stem of green silk holly with five 4" long sprigs
    of six 1"–2½" long leaves and one 1½" clus-
    ter of many ¼" wide red berries
1 oz. of green preserved salal leaves
seventeen 1"–1½" long pine cones
five 9"–11" long pheasant feathers
12" of 24-gauge
    wire
low temperature
    glue gun and
    sticks

1   Cut a 36" length of ribbon. Loop it through the wreath opening. Pull the
    ends even and glue them together. With the remaining ribbon, make a
collar bow (see page 21) with two 4½" loops and two 7" tails. Glue the bow at
the top of the ribbon that wraps the wreath. Cut the poinsettia blossom off the
stem and glue it to the center of the bow. Glue a wire hanger to the back of the
ribbon behind the bow.

2   Cut the cedar into 4"–7" sprigs and glue them in a crescent shape, extend-
    ing as shown. Glue five feathers among the cedar, three to the left of the
ribbon and two to the right.

3   Cut the berries into two 4" and two 6" sprigs. Glue one 4" sprig to the
    wreath just right of the ribbon, angled downward. Glue the other sprig at
1:00, angled down as shown. Glue a 6" sprig among
the greenery at 3:00 and 9:00. Cut the holly into
five 4" sprigs; glue them and the individual salal
leaves evenly spaced among the greenery, following
the angels of the cedar.

4   Glue three pine cones around the poinsettia
    blossom, in clusters of 2–3 at the left and right
of where the ribbon wraps the wreath. Glue the
remaining pine cones evenly spaced among the
greenery. Cut the raspberries into four 4" sprigs and
glue two on each side of the wreath as shown.

13"x16" oval flat open-weave vine wreath
2¾ yards of 1½" wide blue/red/green plaid ribbon
1 stem of green vinyl pine with thirty-six 5" long sprigs
1 red latex poinsettia pick with one 5" wide blossom, four ½" wide red berries and three 1½" long leaves
1 stem of red frosted latex grapes with three 3" long clusters of many ¼"–½" wide grapes
1 stem of blue latex mini berries with eighteen 1" wide berry clusters
1 stem of white latex mini berries with twenty-seven 1" wide berry clusters
2 oz. of white preserved heather
two 2" long blue mushroom birds
12" of 24-gauge wire
low temperature glue gun and sticks

Blue Tartan Wreath

1 Use the ribbon to make two loopy bows (see page 19), each with six 2" loops and two 12" tails. Glue one bow to the wreath at 1:00 and one at 8:00. Weave the tails through the vine as shown and glue to secure.

2 Cut seven 3"–4" sprigs from the lower area of the pine stem and glue them evenly around the upper bow. Cut the remainder into two equal pieces and glue one above and one below the lower bow; angled to follow the wreath as shown. Cut the stem off the poinsettia pick and glue it to the center of the lower bow.

3 Cut the grapes into three 4" sprigs. Glue one at the center of the upper bow, extending downward. Glue one on each side of the lower bow. Cut the blue mini berries into eighteen 1" sprigs and glue them among the greenery around each bow as shown.

4 Cut the white mini berries into nine 4" sprigs, each with three clusters; glue eight sprigs evenly among the greenery around the lower bow. Cut the remaining sprig into three clusters and glue around the upper bow as shown. Cut the heather into 3" sprigs and glue evenly spaced among the greenery. Glue one bird to the center of the upper bow. Glue the other bird at the center bottom of the wreath. Attach a wire hanger (see page 12) at the top back of the wreath.

French Horn Wreath

13" grapevine wreath
3 yards of 1¼" wide red
    velvet ribbon with gold
    wired edges
1 stem of red latex grapes
    with seven 3"–4" long
    sprays of many ¼"
    wide grapes
4 oz. of green preserved
    cedar
2 oz. of white preserved
    heather
2 oz. of gold dried
    Siberian statice
nine 1½" long pine cones
one 5" long gold plastic
    French horn ornament
4 gift picks, each with
    three ½" wide gold foil
    wrapped gift boxes
12" of 24-gauge wire
low temperature glue gun
    and sticks

1 Use the ribbon to make a puffy bow (see page 20) with six 4" loops, two 12" and two 16" tails. Glue the bow to the center top of the wreath. Arrange the tails as shown and glue the ends to secure. Cut the cedar into 6"–8" sprigs and glue them in a crescent shape to extend from under the bow as shown.

2 Glue the French horn to the center of the bow. Cut the red grapes into seven 3" sprigs and glue three to each side of the wreath, evenly spaced. Glue the remaining sprig above the bow center, angled upward.

3 Cut the statice into 4"–6" sprigs and glue the statice and the pine cones evenly spaced among the cedar.

4 Cut the white heather into 5" sprigs and glue at similar angles among the cedar. Glue two gift picks on each side of the wreath spaced 4" apart as shown. Attach a wire hanger (see page 12) at the top back of the wreath.

Poinsettias with Plaid

22" green vinyl pine wreath

3¾ yards of 2½" wide
    red/green/black plaid ribbon with
    gold wired edges

3 red silk poinsettia picks, each with
    one 6" wide blossom and ten ¼"
    berries

2 stems of red frosted latex grapes,
    each with three 1¼" wide clus-
    ters of many ½" wide grapes

6 stems of white silk gypsophila, each
    with two 3" wide clusters of many
    ¼" wide blossoms

1 stem of green latex holly with four
    3" long sprigs, each with three to
    five ¼" wide berries and two to
    seven 1"–2" long leaves

eight 2" long pine cones

2 oz. of green preserved Austral or
    rabbit's foot fern

2 oz. of white dried German statice

12" of 24-gauge wire

low temperature glue gun and sticks

1 Cut each poinsettia with a 1" stem and glue them to the wreath as shown. Use the ribbon to make a puffy bow (see page 20) with a center loop, ten 4" loops, one 20" tail and one 30" tail. Glue the bow at 10:00; arrange and glue the tails among the pine sprigs as shown.

2 Cut the holly into four 4" long sprigs and seven individual leaves; glue the sprigs and leaves evenly spaced among the greenery. Cut the German statice into 4" sprigs and glue evenly spaced among the greenery as shown.

3 Cut the frosted grapes stems into six 4" sprigs and glue them and the pine cones evenly spaced among the greenery.

4 Cut the gypsophila into twelve 3" sprigs and the fern into 5" sprigs. Moving clockwise, glue them evenly spaced among the greenery, alternately extending them toward the inside and outside of the wreath as shown. Attach a wire hanger (see page 12) at the top back of the wreath.

Apples In Gold Wreath

22" green vinyl pine wreath
3⅓ yards of 3½" wide red/gold/green plaid ribbon with gold wired edges
3¼ yards of ⅝" wide gold checked lamé ribbon
eight 2½" wide red latex apples
2 stems of red latex grapes, each with one 5" long cluster of many ¾" wide grapes and two to three 2"–3" long leaves
2 stems of red latex mini berries, each with nine 6" sprigs of six ¾" long berry clusters
1 stem of red latex buds with five 9" sprigs of seven ½" long teardrop-shaped buds
2 oz. of gold preserved bear grass
12" of 24-gauge wire
low temperature glue gun and sticks

1 Use the plaid ribbon to make a puffy bow (see page 20) with four 6" loops, two 6" and two 26" tails. Glue the bow at 1:00; bend the 6" tails to angle up and down and shape the two 26" tails to follow the curve of the wreath. Wire the left tail to the wreath at 10:00 and 8:00; wire the right tail at 4:00; glue to secure. Use the lamé ribbon to make two standup bows (see page 19), each with four 4" loops and one 26" tail. Glue them to the center of the plaid bow, then drape and glue the tails as shown.

2 Glue two apples to the center of the plaid bow and two apples at each point where the tail is wired. Cut each 5" grape cluster in half to form four 2½" clusters; glue one by each apple group, angled as shown.

3 Cut each red mini berry stem into nine 6" sprigs with six clusters each; cut two of these sprigs into three smaller sprigs. Glue the larger sprigs evenly near the apple/grape clusters as shown, then glue the smaller sprigs to fill any empty spaces. Cut the red buds into five 9" sprigs; glue two into the large bow, crossing over the apples as shown. Glue one sprig by each remaining apple cluster.

4 Tuck the tail ends of the right ribbon into the greenery and glue secure. Cut the bear grass into 16" sprigs. Hold together 2–4 sprigs and glue one end to the outside edge of the wreath; cross it to the inside of the wreath and glue to secure. Continue to "wrap" the wreath with sprigs of bear grass as shown above. Make a wire hanger (see page 12) at the top back of the wreath.

Iced Eucalyptus

18" preserved eucalyptus/cedar/box-wood wreath

1 ⅓ yards of 2⅝" wide silver/champagne sheer ribbon with wired edges

1 stem of frosted green vinyl pine with seven 6" sprigs sprayed with snow and glitter

1 stem of blue latex berries with six 6" long sprigs of five ½" wide berries

2 oz. of dried twigs, sprayed silver

1 oz. of dried holly with 2"–4" long leaves, sprayed silver

three 1½"–2½" long pine cones

silver glitter spray

newspapers

12" of 24-gauge wire

low temperature glue gun and sticks

1   Lay the wreath on newspaper; spray it with silver glitter, holding the can about 10" away. Let it dry. Use the ribbon to make an oblong bow (see page 20) with a center loop, two 3" loops, two 4" loops and two 8" tails. Glue the bow to the wreath at 5:00. Attach a wire hanger (see page 12) at the top back of the wreath.

2   Cut the pine pick into seven 6" sprigs and glue them on the right side of the wreath, extending upward above the bow as shown. Cut the twigs into 6"–8" sprigs and glue them evenly spaced among the pine sprigs, angled upward above the bow.

3   Cut the berries into 6" sprigs and glue them above the bow evenly spaced among the pine and twigs. Cut the holly leaves from the stem and glue them evenly spaced among the pine, twigs and berries.

4   Spray the pine cones lightly with the glitter. Let dry and glue as shown above.

Golden Star Wreath

20" green vinyl pine wreath
3⅔ yards of 1½" wide brown taffeta ribbon with gold wired edges
2 stems of gold latex grapes with three 4" long clusters of many ¼"–½" wide grapes
6 oz. of preserved holly, sprayed with gold glitter
4 oz. of brown preserved eucalyptus, sprayed with gold glitter
3 oz. of white preserved rice flower
three 4" wide gold metal mesh stars
three 3" wide gold balls ornament
3 yards of gold bead garland
gold glitter spray
newspapers
12" of 24-gauge wire
low temperature glue gun and sticks

1 Lay the eucalyptus on the newspaper and spray with the gold glitter spray. Let dry. Cut a 25" length of ribbon and set aside. With the rest of the ribbon, make a puffy bow (see page 20) with six 4" loops, one 32" tail and one 24" tail. Glue the bow as shown. Arrange and glue the 32" tail to weave back and forth on the left side of the wreath; repeat with the 24" tail on the right. Glue one end of the 25" ribbon length at 1:00 and weave it among the pine, gluing the other end at 6:00.

2 Cut the bead garland into three 9", three 10" and three 11" lengths. Hold one of each length together; wire them together at each end. Repeat for two more sets, then arrange as shown and glue to the wreath to secure. Glue the stars and ornament balls in trianglular patterns as shown.

3 Cut the rice flower into 3" sprigs and glue them among the pine branches around the wreath, following the same angles. Cut the grapes into six 4" sprigs and glue them evenly spaced around the wreath.

4 Cut the holly into 5" sprigs and glue them evenly spaced among the greenery. Cut the eucalyptus into 5" sprigs and glue evenly spaced clockwise as shown in the large photo. Attach a wire hanger (see page 12) at the top back of the wreath.

Snow Glazed Crescent

22" green vinyl pine wreath

4¼ yards of 2½" wide green/gold ribbon printed with cherubs

3 stems of green vinyl fir picks, each with a
16" section of twenty-five 6" long sprigs

2 stems of snow-glazed latex magnolia picks,
each with a 18"section of one 5" and one 4"
wide burgundy magnolia blossom, one 2"
green apple, one 1½" long pine cone, one
1½" latex brown acorn, two 1" wide yellow
berries and many 4"–7" long green leaves

2 stems of burgundy latex skimmia, each with
three 3" long clusters and one 1½" long
cluster of many berries

2 oz. of dried birch or buck twigs

gold spray paint

newspapers

12" of 24-gauge wire

low temperature glue gun and sticks

1 Lay the birch twigs on the newspaper and
spray with gold paint. Let them dry. Cut two
of the fir stems to 16". Glue one to the left side of
the wreath to extend upward from 8:00 to 11:00.
Glue the other to extend downward from 7:00 to
6:00 and off the wreath. Cut the third pine pick
into twenty-five 6" sprigs and glue them between
the first two stems, extending forward among the
sprigs to create a crescent shape as shown.

2 Cut the magnolia stems to 18". Glue one at
9:00 and one at 8:00, extending downward following the lines of the fir stems.

3 Use the ribbon to make a puffy bow (see page
20) with a center loop, six 5½" loops and two
40" tails. Glue the bow between the magnolia picks
and weave one tail among each floral pick as shown.

4 Cut the skimmia into eight 5" sprigs with one
cluster of berries on each. Glue one above the
center bow loop, one to the lower left of the bow
and three among each stem of magnolias. Cut the
twigs into 6"–8" sprigs and glue them evenly
among the florals and bow as shown. Attach a wire
hanger (see page 12) at the top back of the wreath.

Reva's Wreath

22" round Styrofoam® wreath
2½ yards of 2½" wide bur-
 gundy/green/gold tapestry
 fabric ribbon with gold wired
 edges
6 oz. of gray excelsior
100–110 assorted 1½"–3"
 wide pine and spruce cones
8 holiday picks, each with a 2"
 long red pine cone, a 1"
 wide burgundy rose, a 1"
 wide burgundy/gold foil
 wrapped gift, a 2½" cluster
 of gold branches, three 2"
 long green leaves and three
 2" long vinyl pine sprigs
clear gloss acrylic spray
monofilament nylon fishing line
one paddle of 22-gauge wire
low temperature glue gun and
 sticks

1 Cover the wreath with excelsior and spiral-wrap the wreath with nylon line to secure. Cut a 20" length of wire and wrap one end around the wreath top to form a 2" loop at the top back. Wrap the remaining wire around the wreath.

2 Trim one side of a cone to fit against the inside of the wreath. Cut a 6" length of wire and wrap it around the cone center; twist close to the cone to secure, leaving the wire ends extending on the cut side. Dip the wire ends in glue and insert into the wreath. Repeat to cover the inside, then the out-side of the wreath with cones.

3 Repeat step 2 to completely cover the wreath front. Spray the wreath with gloss acrylic. Let dry and spray again.

4 Use the ribbon to make a puffy bow (see page 20) with a cen-ter loop, six 5" loops and two 11" tails. Glue the bow to the center top of the wreath. Insert the holiday picks through the cones into the foam, as shown in the large photo spacing them evenly.

Burgundy Rose Wreath

18" dark green/burgundy preserved salal wreath

2 yards of 2½" wide burgundy/metallic gold ribbon with gold wired edges

4 stems of burgundy silk roses, each with one 3" wide blossom

2 stems of gold latex mini berries, each with eighteen 2½" long clusters of many ⅛" wide berries

2 stems of red/burgundy latex raspberries, each with 2 clusters of three 1" wide berries and one 1" wide berry

2 stems of purple latex grapes, each with three 2½"–3" long clusters of many ¼"–½" wide grapes

3 holiday picks, each with a 1" wide burgundy foil wrapped gift, a 1" wide burgundy apple, 3" long cluster of twelve ¼" wide burgundy grapes and four 2"–3" long leaves

3 oz. of green preserved Austral or rabbit's foot fern

2 oz. of burgundy dried glittered German statice

12" of 24-gauge wire

low temperature glue gun and sticks

1 Use the ribbon to make an oblong bow (see page 20) with a center loop, two 3½" loops, four 4" loops and two 8" tails. Glue the bow to the bottom wreath front. Cut the roses to 4" and glue as shown.

2 Cut the holiday pick stems to 2" and glue evenly spaced between the roses. Cut the Austral fern into 5" sprigs and glue them evenly spaced around the wreath, alternately angling the sprigs to the outside and inside.

3 Cut each stem of the gold mini berry into eighteen 4" sprigs and glue them evenly spaced around the wreath. Cut the raspberries into four 3" sprigs; twist the stems of the two single berries together to form a sprig. Glue all five sprigs evenly around the wreath as shown.

4 Cut the grapes into six 4" sprigs and glue them evenly spaced around the wreath. Cut the glittered German statice into 5" sprigs. Glue 2–3 sprigs around the center bow as shown in the large photo. Glue the remaining sprigs evenly spaced around the wreath. Attach a wire hanger (see page 12) at the top back of the wreath.

Tabletop Treasures

Centerpieces can be designed to be placed against a wall or in the center of a table. When designed for the table, elements of the piece must be positioned to be viewed from all sides. However, if it is to be displayed against a wall, just three sides are viewed, making construction a bit simpler.

Another consideration before constructing a tabletop design is the size and shape of the area to be filled. Measuring the space beforehand prevents creating a piece that is out of scale or doesn't fit the area adequately.

Several centerpieces featured in this section begin with a purchased pine or fir pre-formed base. These can be found with a center hole, providing space for a candle, or with a solid center area. The latter can be decorated either for a tabletop or, more creatively, as a swag for the wall.

In most instances, an object which sits on the table can be made into a tabletop floral decoration; usually it just takes space on the piece where floral foam can be attached. We've made creating tabletop treasures as easy and fool-proof as possible, yet included some spectacular pieces to help deck your home for the holidays.

12"x7"x2½" rectangular wood planter box
1 ½ yards of 2½" wide red/white/green plaid ribbon
   with wired edges
8 oz. of 2"–4" long red dried chilis
6 oz. of dried lilac beauty achillia
5 oz. of dried barley
3 oz. of dried brisa media
3 oz. of dried phleum grass
2 oz. of dried black-bearded wheat

2 oz. of mood moss
two 2½" wide dried lotus pods
one 6" wide dried sponge mushroom
one 3"x4"x8" and one 2"x2" square of floral foam for
   silks and drieds
serrated knife
24" of 24-gauge wire
low temperature glue gun and sticks

1 Use the serrated knife to cut the foam to fit inside the planter and glue
   to secure. Cut the brisa media to 16"–18" and wire the stems together in
the center of the bunch. Repeat for the phleum grass. Lay the brisa media
diagonally across the planter as shown. Lift at the stems and glue a 2"x4"x1"
foam piece under the bunch at the wiring. Glue the brisa media to the foam
square, then glue the phleum diagonally across the brisa as shown.

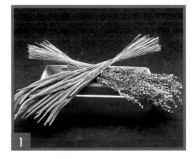

2 Wire the barley together just under the heads. Cut the bunch to 8" and
   glue it into the foam extending upward in front of the point the brisa
and phleum cross. Use the ribbon to make an oblong bow (see page 20) with
a center loop, two 3" loops, two 4" loops and two 10" tails. Glue the bow to
the foam angled as shown. Wire the lilac achillia together and cut the bunch
to 8". Glue it to the foam, extending left as shown.

3 Wire the wheat together and cut the stems to 7". Glue it to the foam in
   front of and angled in the same direction as the phleum grass. Insert
one-third of the chilis into the foam, between the phleum grass and the
wheat. Insert the remaining two-thirds of the chilis into the foam at the back
right, between the brisa media and the barley.
Cut the lotus pod stems to 3" and glue them on
each side of the bow as shown.

4 Glue the sponge mushroom to the back
   left of the arrangement, extending upward
between the achillia and the barley. Break the
moss into 1"–2" tufts and glue them around the
bow, filling empty spaces and hiding exposed
foam.

22" high green vinyl pine tree with burlap-
    wrapped base
nine 32" long strands of raffia
1 stem of red latex mini berries with eighteen
    1½"-2" clusters of many ⅛" berries
2 stems of red/orange latex bittersweet, each
    with a 12" and a 14" long sprig of many
    clusters of three to six ¼" wide berries
14 pine cone picks, each with four ½" long
    flocked pine cones and five ¼" long
    teardrop-shaped red berries
3 oz. of white dried German statice
3 oz. of white dried lichen
five 1" long green/yellow mushroom birds
eight 1" wide brown fiber bird nests
one 3¾" wide papier-mâché star
low temperature glue gun and sticks

Prairie
Pine
Tree

1 Glue the star to the tree top as shown. Cut the bittersweet into many
   clusters of 3–6 berries and glue them evenly spaced among the branches
as shown.

2 Cut the mini berries into eighteen 1½"-2" sprigs, each with a ¾" stem.
   Glue them evenly spaced among the tree branches. Cut the German statice
into 2"–3" sprigs. Glue them evenly spaced among the branches. Glue the ends
of four raffia strands at the base of the star and wrap them downward around the
tree with the wraps 3"-4" apart. When coming to the ends of these strands, glue
four more strands to the ends of the first strands and continue to the bottom
branches of the tree. Glue the ends into the lower branches to secure.

3 Break the lichen into 2" tufts and glue them evenly spaced among the
   tree branches. Cut the pine cone picks to 1" and
   glue them evenly spaced among all the branches.

4 Glue a bird at the top left and middle right of
   the tree front as shown in large photo. Glue
one bird nest at the lower left and glue one bird
into the nest. Glue the other two birds to the back
side of the tree, 4" above and below the mid-point.
Glue the remaining bird nests evenly scattered
among the pine branches. Wrap the remaining
strand of raffia around the base and tie in a shoestring bow (see page 18) with 2" loops and 3" tails.

Woodland Angel Centerpiece

11"x 5½"x2½" pine box
one 13" tall woodland angel with a red cape,
  pine halo, a rose/pine cone garland and a
  pine and rose sprig on the bottom cape
  edge
2 stems of green vinyl pine, each with nine-
  teen 5" long sprigs
3 stems of ivory latex roses, each with one
  2" wide blossom
2 stems of red latex grapes, each with two 4"
  long clusters of many ½" wide grapes
4 oz. of green preserved blueberry juniper
twenty-four 25" long raffia strands
2 oz. of red glittered dried German statice
2 oz. of white preserved baby's breath
2 oz. of gold dried Siberian statice
1 oz. of green dried sphagnum moss
one 3"x4"x8" block of floral foam for silks
  and drieds
12" of 24-gauge wire
low temperature glue gun and sticks

1 Glue the foam block into the center of the
  box, then trim the foam flush with the box
rim. Break the moss into small tufts and glue them
between the foam and box sides and to the outside
of the box as shown. Glue the angel to the left end
of the foam.

2 Cut the pine into 5" sprigs; glue them into the
  foam with two sprigs in each corner of the left
end. Cut one rose stem to 10", one to 7" and one to
5". Glue the 10" stem into the back of the foam,
just right of the angel. Glue the 7" sprig to the far
right end of the foam and the 5" stem to the front,
just right of the angel, angled forward. Cut the
juniper into 4"–6" sprigs and insert them evenly
spaced among the greenery.

3 Hold the raffia strands together and cut in half
  to make two 12" bundles. Fold a bundle in half
to form a 6" loop (see page 21) and wire the ends
together to secure. Use fingernails to shred the
loops. Repeat to make a second set of loops. Glue
one loop set on each side of the angel. Cut the
grapes into four 5" sprigs and glue them among the
pine. Cut the German statice into 5" sprigs and
glue them evenly spaced among the greenery.

4 Cut the Siberian statice into 5"–10" sprigs and
  glue them evenly spaced throughout the
design with the taller sprigs toward the back. Cut
the baby's breath into 6" sprigs and glue them
evenly spaced among the florals and greenery.

Holiday Chair

6"x12"x5½" red painted wooden chair
1¼ yards of ⅞" wide red/green plaid ribbon
6 stems of 1" wide burgundy dried roses
five 1½" long pine cones
3 oz. of green preserved cedar
3 oz. of white preserved ti-tree
1 oz. of dried rice grass
1 oz. of green dried sphagnum moss
2"x2"x2" block of floral foam for silks and drieds
metallic gold spray paint
newspapers
12" of 24-gauge wire
low temperature glue gun and sticks

1   Place the pine cones on the newspapers and spray with the gold paint. Let dry. Glue the foam to the back left corner of the chair seat. Cut the cedar into 3"–6" sprigs and glue them into the foam, with the 6" sprigs at the top and diagonally across the seat as shown. Glue the shorter sprigs filling the area between.

2   Glue moss to cover the back of the foam. In the front, glue small tufts of moss to cover any exposed foam between the cedar sprigs. Use the ribbon to make an oblong bow (see page 20) with a center loop, two 2" loops, two 2½" loops and two 10" tails. Glue the bow to the cedar at the back left corner of the chair, just above the arm.

3   Cut the roses into 3½" sprigs and insert them into the foam in an inverted triangle shape as shown. Cut the ti-tree into 4"–6" sprigs and glue them evenly spaced near materials of similar lengths.

4   Glue the pine cones evenly spaced among the rose blossoms. Cut the rice grass into 4"–6" sprigs and glue them evenly spaced throughout the florals and greenery. Arrange the bow tails across the chair arms as shown and glue to secure.

Teddy Bear Sleigh

12"x4"x5½" red/green wood and wire sleigh
1⅔ yards of 1⅜" wide red/green plaid ribbon
1 stem of red silk anemones with five 6" sprigs,
    each with one 2" wide blossom
1 green latex holly bush with five 6" long
    branches, each with a cluster of ½"–¾" wide
    red berries three to five 2"–3" long leaves
8 oz. of green preserved Frazier fir
3 oz. of dried artemesia
2 oz. of green dried sphagnum moss
five 2"–2½" long pine cones
one 6" tall jointed burlap bear
1 gift pick with three ¾"–1¼" wide white
    wrapped stacked gift boxes, tied with red
    satin ribbon
3"x4"x8" brick of floral foam for silks and
    drieds
serrated knife
12" of 24-gauge wire
low temperature glue gun and sticks

1 Cut the foam to fit inside the sleigh, leaving a ½" space between the foam and sides; glue in place. Insert moss between the foam and basket sides and cover the top to conceal the foam. Bend the bear into a sitting position and glue it to the front of the basket, angled as shown.

2 Cut the Frazier fir into 6"–10" sprigs and insert them into the foam in a triangular shape as shown with the tallest sprigs at the back and the shortest in front. Cut the holly into five sprigs: one 10", one 4" and three 6". Insert the sprigs into the foam among the fir, positioning them near sprigs of similar lengths.

3 Cut the artemesia into 6"–10" sprigs and glue them evenly spaced throughout the arrangement as for the holly. Cut the anemones into five 6"–10" sprigs and glue them among the florals as shown.

4 Use the ribbon to make an oblong bow (see page 20) with a center loop, two 2" loops, four 2½" loops, two 3" loops, one 7" tail and one 8" tail. Glue the bow to the rim of the sleigh, near the left end. Arrange the tails as shown and glue them to the sleigh to secure. Cut the stem off the stacked gift pick and glue it into the bear's lap. Glue the pine cones among the florals as shown. Cut the rice grass into 6"–10" sprigs and insert them evenly spaced near sprigs of similar lengths.

Centerpiece with Protea

6"x4"x2½" green plastic floral bowl

2⅔ yards of 1⅜" wide burgundy/green/black tapestry ribbon

5 stems of green vinyl pine, each with three 8" branches of seven 5" long sprigs

3 stems of gilded burgundy poinsettias, each with one 7" wide blossom and two 4" long gilded leaves

1 stem of green latex mum leaves with five 5" sprig of two or three 3" long leaves and a 7" sprig of six 3" long leaves

2 stems of burgundy latex cranberries, each with two 3" wide and one 2" wide clusters of many ¼" berries

five 4" long dried protea flowers

fifteen 1"–2" long pine cones

3"x4"x6" block of floral foam for silks and drieds

12" of 24-gauge wire

low temperature glue gun and sticks

1 Glue the foam into the bowl. Cut the pine stems into fifteen 8" branches, then cut three of the branches in half. Glue the sprigs into the foam with the longer branches on the ends and the shorter branches at the front and back forming an oval shape.

2 Cut the poinsettia stems to 3" and insert them into the foam as shown. Cut the six poinsettia leaves off the stems and glue them evenly spaced among the pine branches. Cut the mum leaves into five 5" sprigs and one 7" sprig; cut the 7" sprig in half. Glue the sprigs evenly spaced throughout the arrangement.

3 Cut the cranberries into three 5" sprigs each with a cluster of berries, then cut each sprig in half to make six sprigs with a half-cluster of berries each. Glue the sprigs evenly spaced among the pine. Cut the protea flower into 6" sprigs. Glue one at top center, angled to the right and glue two to each long side of the centerpiece toward the ends of the piece.

4 Glue the pine cones evenly spaced throughout the design. Cut four 12" lengths of ribbon; trim the tails diagonally. With the remaining ribbon, make a standup bow (see page 19) with five 4½" loops. Glue the bow just to the right of top center, angled as shown. Glue one end of the four ribbon lengths around the bow, then weave the tails among the pine to extend toward the ends of the centerpiece.

Dried Rose Arrangement

6"x4" round gold-brushed wicker basket
1 stem of white silk baby's breath with two 10" sprigs of 5 and one 6" sprig of three 1½" wide clusters of many ¹⁄₁₆" wide blossoms and many 2" long leaves
6 oz. of green preserved Frazier fir
2 oz. of dried birch twigs
4 oz. of green preserved cedar
10 stems of 1" wide red dried roses
ten 1½"–2½" long gold pine cones
two 10" long sticks of dried cinnamon
2 oz. of green sphagnum moss
3"x4"x8" block of floral foam for silks and drieds
serrated knife
metallic gold spray paint, newspapers
low temperature glue gun and sticks

1 Lay the birch twigs on the newspaper and spray with the gold paint. Let dry. Cut the foam to fit the basket; leave 1" extending above the basket rim. Glue the foam in the basket. Cut the fir into 6"–14" sprigs and glue them into the foam in a tri-angular shape as shown with a 14" sprig extending upward, one to the right and one to the left. Cut the twigs into 12" and 15" sprigs and glue them into the center back of the foam as shown. Cut the cedar into 4"–10" sprigs and glue among the fir near materials of similar lengths.

2 Cut the roses into ten 3"-12" sprigs. Glue them into the foam in a tall triangular shape with the longest in the back. Break the moss into 2"–4" tufts. Glue a 4" tuft to conceal the foam at the back of the arrangement. Glue 2" tufts into the arrangement to cover any exposed foam.

3 Cut the baby's breath into two 10" sprigs with five blossom clusters, one 4" sprig with two blossom clusters and one 2" sprig with one blossom cluster. Glue a 10" sprig into the foam on each side of the roses. Glue the 4" sprig to the lower left of the arrangement with the blossoms angled downward. Glue the 2" sprig to the lower right of the arrangement.

4 Glue the cinnamon sticks at the bottom front of the arrangement crossed as shown. Glue the pine cones evenly spaced among the baby's breath and roses in the lower two-thirds of the design.

Oval Candle Centerpiece

36" long vinyl pine centerpiece with a 4" wide center opening

2¾ yards of 1⅞" wide red/green/gold music-printed ribbon with gold wired edges

2 stems of red silk poinsettias, each with one 6" wide blossom

4 red latex grape picks, each with one 5" long cluster of many ½" wide grapes and five 2"–3" long leaves

1 stem of silk holly with four 6" sprigs, each with one 1" wide cluster of ½" wide red berries, three to five

2"–3" long leaves and a 4" tendril

3 stems of gold plastic coral with three 7" long branches of four 4"–5" long sprigs

4 oz. of green preserved Frazier fir

3 oz. of dark red glittered dried German statice

one 5" long gold plastic trumpet

one 5½" long gold plastic violin

one 4"x8" gold pillar candle

low temperature glue gun and sticks

1 Fluff the branches of the centerpiece. Cut the gold coral into nine 7" sprigs and glue them evenly spaced among the pine branches. Cut the Frazier fir into 6" sprigs and glue them as for the coral.

2 Cut the poinsettias into 3" sprigs and glue one at each side of the center opening. Cut the ribbon in half. Glue one end of each length at opposite ends of the centerpiece and weave them across the greenery crossing them near each end and on each end of the center hole.

3 Glue an instrument at each end of the centerpiece halfway between the center and the end. Glue one grape pick in front of and one behind each instrument, angled to drape over the edge of the centerpiece.

4 Cut the holly into four 5" sprigs, each with a berry cluster; glue them evenly spaced around the center opening. Cut the German statice into 4" sprigs and glue them evenly spaced among the florals and greenery. Place the candle in the center hole as shown in the large photo.

Basket Trio Centerpiece

3 oval wire/wicker baskets, each 6"x4" with a 5" tall
   handle
1 yard of 1¼" wide red/green plaid ribbon
four 12" long pheasant feathers
1 stem of green silk holly with nine 6" sprigs of six
   1½"–3" long leaves and one 1" long cluster of ¼"
   wide red berries
3 stems of red latex raspberries, each with two 4" sprigs
   of five ½" wide berries and four 1" long leaves

three 2½" wide dried lotus pods
18 stems of dried black-bearded wheat
2 oz. of dried birch twigs
2 oz. of green dried sphagnum moss
3"x4"x8" block of floral foam for silks and drieds
serrated knife
12" of 24-gauge wire
low temperature glue gun and sticks

1   Turn the baskets with the long sides touching and angled as shown; wire them together at the upper
and lower rims. Cut the foam into thirds and glue one into each basket. Fill the spaces around the foam
with moss.

2   Cut the twigs into 12" sprigs. Divide in half, then wire the bundles together with the ends overlapping forming a 23" long bunch. Glue and wire this bunch centered over the handle top of the middle
basket, extending toward the outer basket handles. Cut the wheat into eigh-
teen 4" sprigs, wire in clusters of three and glue into the basket as shown.

3   Glue the feathers to the handle top of the center basket, two feathers
facing right and two facing left. Cut the holly into nine 4" sprigs and
glue three evenly spaced into each basket. Insert one lotus pod into the center of each basket, angled randomly.

4   Use the ribbon to make a Dior bow (see page 19) with two 3½" loops,
two 5" tails and two 6" tails. Wire the bow to the handle top of the center basket; glue to
reinforce. Cut the
raspberries into
six 4" sprigs and
glue two into
each basket as
shown.

Folk Santa Candleholder

one 4½"x3" round wicker basket

one 7" tall red/white/green metal candleholder with a
  6" wide flying Santa

2 stems of green vinyl pine, each with twenty-one 4"
  long pine sprigs

1 stem of flocked green vinyl pine with fourteen 4"
  long pine sprigs

3 stems of red latex raspberries, each with two 3"
  long sprigs of five ½" berries and four 1" leaves

1 stem of white latex berries with nine 4" long sprigs
  of three 1" wide clusters of many 1/16" wide berries

2 stems of red latex tear-shaped berries, each with
  five 8" sprigs of six ½" long berries

3 oz. of white dried German statice

nine 2" long flocked pine cones

one 3"x4"x8" block of floral foam for silks and drieds

serrated knife

one 12" tall red taper candle

low temperature glue gun and sticks

1 Cut the foam to fit the basket and glue it in
  place. Set the candleholder centered on the
foam and press down to make a mark where it
will be glued in step 2. Cut the green pine sprigs
off the main stem and insert 26 sprigs into the foam around the basket curving
over the rim as shown. Insert the remaining sprigs into the middle of the foam,
leaving the marked circle exposed.

2 Glue the candle holder into the center of the foam. Cut the flocked pine
  stem into fourteen 4" sprigs and glue them evenly spaced among the greenery. Glue the pine cones evenly spaced, angled outward throughout the greenery.

3 Cut the white berries into nine 3" sprigs with two clusters and nine 2"
  sprigs with one cluster. Glue the sprigs evenly spaced among the greenery.
Cut the raspberries into six 5" sprigs. Glue one to each side of the arrangement
and two each at the front and back, angled as shown.

4 Cut the statice into
  4" sprigs and glue
them evenly spaced
among the greenery. Cut
the tear-shaped berry
stems into ten 8" sprigs
with six berries each.
Insert them into the
foam, evenly spaced
around base of the candle
holder. Angle the sprigs
outward and downward.

Potpourri Birdfeeder

7"x7"x9" wood bird
   feeder with a
   glass front
1⅓ yards of ⅝"
   wide gold lamé
   ribbon
1 stem of burgundy
   latex berries with
   four 4" long
   sprigs of five ½"
   wide berries
4 oz. of green pre-
   served Frazier fir
12 oz. of burgundy/
   green/white pot-
   pourri
maple spray stain
white spray paint
matte finish spray
   sealer
soft cloth
newspaper
6" of 24-gauge wire
low temperature
   glue gun and
   sticks

1. Tape off the glass front of the birdfeeder. Spray maple stain over the entire birdfeeder and use a soft cloth to wipe off the excess. Let dry. Spray the birdfeeder with clear sealer and let dry completely; then spray the entire roof white (protect all the birdfeeder but the rooftop with newspapers). Remove the tape from the glass and fill the birdfeeder and tray with potpourri.

2. Cut the Frazier fir into 4" sprigs and set half the sprigs aside for step 4. Lightly mist the remaining fir sprigs with white paint for a snowy effect.

3. Glue three sprayed fir sprigs to the roof at the top left, angled as shown. Glue one sprig to the wood frame on each side of the glass. Cut the berries into four 4" sprigs. Glue one among the fir on each side of the glass and the other two among the fir sprigs on the roof.

4. Cut the unsprayed fir sprigs in 2" pieces and glue evenly spaced among the sprayed fir sprigs. Cut the ribbon into three 6" and one 27" length. Use two 6" lengths to make two collar bows (see page 21), each with two 1" loops and two 1" tails. Glue one bow at the base of each fir sprig in the feeder tray. Use the 27" length to make an oblong bow (see page 20) with a center loop, four 1½" loops and two 4" tails. Glue it to the top left roof peak as shown in the large photo. Cut the remaining 6" ribbon length into ¼" squares and mix the pieces among the potpourri.

Terra Cotta Trio

one 4½" tall terra cotta flower pot

two 3½" tall terra cotta flower pots

2 yards of ⅞" wide dark red/green/tan tapestry ribbon

4 oz. of green preserved cedar

4 oz. of green preserved blueberry juniper

4 oz. of green preserved boxwood

5 oz. of dried barley

4 oz. of red dried pepper berries

2 oz. of dried rice grass

eighteen 1½" long pine cones

two 1" wide candle cups

three 12" tall burgundy taper candles

one 3"x4"x8" block of floral foam for silks and drieds

serrated knife

12" of 24 gauge wire

low temperature glue gun and sticks

1 Cut the floral foam into one 5"x5" and two 3"x3" squares. Trim each square and glue into the pots. Trim off any foam showing above the rims. Insert a candle cup into the center of each foam square in the small pots. Cut ⅓ of the cedar into 3" sprigs and the remaining ⅔ into 4"–6" sprigs. Glue the 3" sprigs into both small pots and the 4"–6" sprigs into the large pot extending upward and outward as shown.

2 Cut the juniper into 3" and 4"–6" sprigs in the same proportions as for the cedar. Glue the sprigs evenly spaced among the cedar, dividing the 3" sprigs between the two small pots. Cut and glue the boxwood as for the juniper.

3 Cut 18 sprigs of barley into 3" sprigs and glue nine sprigs, in clusters of three, evenly spaced among the greenery in each small pot. Cut the remaining barley into twenty-five 6" sprigs and five 4" sprigs. Glue the 6" sprigs around the edge of the large pot in five clusters of three at 45° angles. Glue a 4" sprig between the clusters. Cut the pepper berries into 1"–3" sprigs and glue them evenly spaced among the florals in all three pots.

4 Glue five pine cones evenly spaced in each small pot; glue the remaining cones in the larger pot. Cut ⅓ of the rice grass into 3½" sprigs; glue half of these sprigs evenly spaced into each small pot. Cut the remaining ⅔ of the rice grass into 5"–7" sprigs; glue them evenly spaced among the greenery in the larger pot. Wrap ribbon around the rim of each pot and glue. Cut the remaining ribbon into two 12" lengths and one 14" length. With each shorter length, make a shoestring bow (see page 18) with two 2" loops and 2" tails. Use the longer length to make a shoestring bow with two 2" loops and 3" tails. Glue the bows to the pot rims as shown in the large photo.

Great GARLANDS & Sensational SWAGS

Because of their size, garlands and swags provide a feeling of celebration at Christmas. Their textures and unusual shapes add interest to the decorated home. Garlands can be long and luxurious, draped elegantly down a staircase or displayed over a fireplace mantel. And swags can be made in a variety of shapes to fill certain areas on walls or doors.

When working with garlands questions of the placement of decorations and floral elements can be answered by first "trying the garland on for size." Before decorating it, hang or place it where it is intended to be when finished. Determine its shape, how many drapes will be formed if it's to be looped, whether the ends should be bent downward, etc. This will help decide the locations of the floral elements and bows and avoid mistakes. After fitting it to the space, attach wire hangers to the back in the appropriate places for the garland to hang properly.

Swags can start with a greenery, grapevine or even a twig base. Many different looks and appearances are achieved, from woodsy to country to elegant, by adding the appropriate components to the swag bases.

Garlands don't have to remain as long, slender bases. If a greenery swag base proves difficult to find, a garland can be cut into lengths, then wired together to form the desired shape. Cut garland pieces can be used to decorate many different bases because of their flexibility; many times this is more economical than using individual greenery stems.

Garlands and swags are fun to work with and provide a strong statement in any setting at Christmas time.

Rose Garland

5' long green vinyl pine garland
2 yards of 3" wide gold sheer ribbon
 with gold wired edges
one 52" white/pink silk rose garland
 with twenty-four 1"–4" wide
 rose blossoms, twenty-six 1"
 wide white dogwood blossoms,
 curling vine tendrils and many
 1"–2" long leaves

6 stems of pearlized white berries,
 each with ten ½"–⅝" wide
 berries, 3 curly tendrils and one
 1" long pine cone
1 stem of gold latex mini-berries
 with twenty-seven 1" wide clusters of many ⅛" berries
2 stems of gold silk lotus leaves,
 each with nine 2"–3" long leaves

4 oz. of gold preserved cedar
2 oz. of dried birch twigs
metallic gold spray paint
newspapers
12" of 24-gauge wire
low temperature glue gun and sticks

1 Place the birch twigs on the paper and spray with gold paint. Let dry. Fluff the branches of the pine garland and center the rose garland on top of it. Wire the garlands together. Add wire hangers (see page 12) to the center back and if desired, 4" away from the end of each side.

2 Weave the ribbon among the roses from one end of the garland to the other; glue to secure. Cut the gold cedar into 5" sprigs and glue evenly among the florals and greenery, extending from the center toward the ends.

3 Cut the pearlized berry stems to 9" and glue three evenly spaced among the florals and greenery, on the left side extending toward the end. Repeat on the right side. Cut the gold mini-berries into nine 4" sprigs and glue evenly spaced throughout the garland.

4 Cut the gold twigs into 8" sprigs and glue among the florals and greenery in clusters of 3–5, angling as shown. Cut the lotus leaves into 4" sprigs and glue evenly among the florals and greenery as shown.

Romantic Garland

9' green vinyl pine garland

7⅔ yards of 2½" wide gold/white checked sheer ribbon with wired edges

two 9' white pearl strings with ¼" pearls

5 stems of pink silk roses, each with one 4" wide blossom

2 stems of pink mini-roses, each with two 2" sprigs of three 1" wide blossoms

4 stems of gold-brushed green latex rose leaves, each with seven 3½" sprigs of three 2½"–3" long leaves

1 stem of gold latex berries with nine 4" sprigs of three 1" wide clusters with many ⅛" wide berries

4 stems of white silk vervain, each with three 7" long blossoms

3 oz. of preserved baby's breath

four 4" round white crocheted doilies

4 angel picks, each with a 2½" tall gold cherub

12" of 24-gauge wire

low temperature glue gun and sticks

1 Bend the garland every 30" to create four draped sections as shown in the large photo. Cut five 32" lengths of ribbon and use each to make a puffy bow (see page 20) with four 4" loops. Drape the remaining ribbon across the garland, leaving a 4" tail at each end. Glue at each bent area to secure and trim the tail ends diagonally. Glue a bow at each end and one at each bent area. Cut the large roses with 1" stems and glue one at the center of each bow.

2 For each doily, gather the doily at the center and wrap wire ½" from the center to secure. Glue one doily at the lowest point of each draped section. Cut the mini roses into 2" sprigs each with one blossom; glue three sprigs at the center of each doily. Glue an angel pick above each doily.

3 Cut the gold-brushed rose leaves into 4" sprigs, each with three leaves, and glue evenly spaced among the greenery, extending toward each end. Cut the gold berries into nine 4" sprigs, each with three berry clusters; glue one just to the left of the center rose and the rest evenly spaced along the garland.

4 Cut the vervain into 7" sprigs and glue three sprigs evenly spaced along each draped area. Cut the baby's breath into 3"–4" sprigs and glue evenly spaced among the florals. Glue one end of each pearl string to each end of the garland. Evenly drape one string behind each large rose, gluing to secure. Evenly drape the other string behind each angel, gluing to secure.

Terra Cotta Fireplace Garland

5' green vinyl pine garland

2 yards of 2½" wide burgundy/olive/gold tapestry ribbon with wired edges

4 stems of burgundy silk statice, each with two 2"–3" long clusters of blossoms

2 stems of grey flocked nuts, each with a 14" section of twelve ¾" wide nuts and many 2½" long leaves

2 stems of latex holly, each with 4 sprigs of six ¼" wide red berries and many 1"–2" long green leaves

1 stem of red latex mini-berries with fifteen 9" sprigs of many ⅛" long berries

4 oz. of light green preserved ti-tree

2 oz. of copper dried holly leaves

2 oz. of light green dried silene grass

five 2" long blue mushroom birds

terra cotta pots: one 3½" wide", two 2½" wide and two 1½" wide

low temperature glue gun and sticks

1 Fluff the sprigs to extend toward each end, then weave the ribbon among the pine for the full length of the garland. Glue the 3½" pot in the center of the garland, with the opening tipped to the right. Glue the 2½" pots 12" to the right and left of the center pot and glue the 1½" pots 12" to the right and left of the medium pots, angled as shown in the large photo. Cut the dried holly leaves into 3" sprigs and glue evenly spaced among the greenery toward each end.

2 Cut the burgundy statice into eight 4" sprigs, each with one blossom, and glue evenly spaced among the greenery angled toward each end. Cut the grey nuts into twelve 4" sprigs, each with two nuts, and glue as for the statice. Cut the latex holly into eight 5" sprigs. Glue evenly spaced among the greens and florals.

3 Cut the ti-tree into 5" sprigs and glue evenly among the greenery, extending toward each end. Cut the silene grass into 5" sprigs and glue evenly spaced among the greenery, as for the ti-tree.

4 Glue the mushroom birds across the garland. Cut the berry spray into fifteen 9" sprigs and glue across the garland, extending toward each end.

Teddy Bear Garland

9' green vinyl pine garland with twenty 2"–2½" pine cones

4½ yards of 2½" wide red/green/cream paper ribbon with holly print

1¼ yards of ⅛" wide red satin ribbon

1 stem of red latex mini-berries with twenty-seven 1" wide clusters of many ⅛" wide berries

5 apple picks, each with six 1"–2" long green/white leaves, one ½" wide apple and two ½" wide apple quarters

3 oz. of preserved baby's breath

six 5" tall stuffed teddy bears with jointed legs and red bows at the necks

one 5½" long gold plastic violin

two 5" long gold plastic trumpets

two 5" long gold plastic French horns

six 2" wide wooden heart cutouts

12" of 24-gauge wire

low temperature glue gun and sticks

1 Wind the paper ribbon clockwise around the length of the garland ten times; glue at the back at each end and each wrap to secure. Bend the arms and legs of the bears into different poses and glue evenly spaced along the garland.

2 Cut the apple picks into 4" sprigs; glue them centered between the bears. Glue the violin at the center of the garland. Glue one trumpet and one horn to the right and left, midway between the violin and the garland ends.

3 Cut the red berries into nine 4" sprigs, each with three clusters of berries, and glue evenly spaced among the greenery. Cut the baby's breath into 4"–5" sprigs and glue evenly spaced among the greenery.

4 Cut the ribbon into six 8" lengths; use each to make a shoestring bow (see page 21) with two 1" loops and two 1½" tails. Glue one bow at the top center of each wooden heart, then glue a heart near each bear.

one 9' green vinyl pine garland with ten 1"–3" pine
   cones
one 36" burgundy silk magnolia swag with eight 4"–6"
   wide blossoms, fourteen 9" sprigs of 1"–2" open
   buds, eight 9" stems of 1" closed buds, many 3"–7"
   leaves, four 6" sprigs of two 1½"–2" wide pink dogwood blossoms and many 3" leaves
3 stems of gold latex grapes, each with three 4" clusters
   of many ¼"–½" grapes
6 oz. of green preserved boxwood
4 oz. of red preserved holly

4 oz. of white preserved ti tree
fifteen 3"–4" long red/white pine cones
low temperature glue gun and sticks

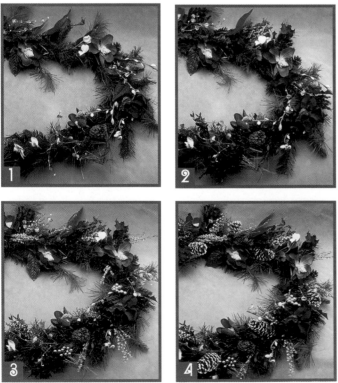

1 Dismantle the magnolia garland so that all the
stems of blossoms and buds are separate. Glue
two of the 6" wide blossoms to the center of the
garland, 3" apart. Glue another 6" wide blossom 7"
to the left and one to the right of these blossoms.
Glue a 4" blossom 7" to the left of the left blossom
and one 7" to the right of the right blossom. Glue
one stem with two 2" buds at each end of the garland. Glue another stem with two 2" buds 30" from
the center on each side. Glue the stems with 1"
open buds around the center four magnolias,
extending toward the outside and the stems with
the 1" closed blossoms evenly around the 4" blossoms on each side.

2 Cut the red holly into 5"–7" sprigs and glue
evenly spaced among the pine, with the sprigs
extending from the center toward each end. Cut
the boxwood into 5"–7" sprigs and repeat.

3 Cut the white ti tree into 4"–7" sprigs. Glue
evenly spaced among the other materials,
angled as for the holly. Cut the grapes into 5" sprigs
and repeat.

4 Glue four of the red/white pine cones around
the center two magnolias, with one extending
to the upper right and one to the lower left. Glue
the rest evenly spaced among the other magnolias.

5' green vinyl pine fireplace garland with twenty 1"–4" long pine cones

3 stems of white silk carnations, each with three 7" long sprigs of one 2" wide blossom and one 1" wide bud

3 stems of burgundy silk heather, each with three 7" long sprigs of many blossoms

1 stem of white latex lilies with three 6"–8" wide blossoms and two 4" long closed buds

7 stems of burgundy silk carnations, each with one 3" wide blossom

1 green silk holly bush with 14 sprigs of six 2"–3" long leaves and 1 cluster of ⅛" wide red berries

2 stems of white silk plum blossoms, each with one 18" and one 10" sprig with 3 sprigs of many 1" wide blossoms and 2" long leaves

six 4" long flocked pine cones

eight 2½" wide gold ball ornaments

low temperature glue gun and sticks

Banquet Garland

1 Arrange the garland with the center pine sprigs extending upward as shown. Cut the burgundy carnations into seven 4" sprigs and glue evenly spaced throughout the center. Cut the heather into nine 7" sprigs and glue among the greenery as shown.

2 Cut the lilies into three 6" sprigs and glue in a triangle as shown, gluing the lily with two buds 7" to the right of center. Cut the white carnations into nine 4" sprigs and glue three around the lilies and the rest evenly spaced among the greenery.

3 Cut the holly bush into fourteen 4" sprigs and glue evenly among the greenery and florals. Glue the flocked pine cones evenly spaced along the garland, angling as shown.

4 Cut the plum blossoms into eight 7" sprigs. Glue evenly among the florals, angling the sprigs from the center toward each end. Glue the ball ornaments evenly spaced among the greenery.

Raffia Garden Garland

8 oz. of raffia with 48" long strands
3 1/3 yards of 2 3/4" wide red/white/green plaid ribbon
   with wired edges
fifteen 2" wide dried apple slices
four 2 1/2" tall tin watering cans
two 2 1/2" tall tin buckets
2 oz. of red dried canella

2 oz. of green preserved cedar
1 oz. of white dried German statice
1 oz. of green dried sphagnum moss
3"x4"x8" block of floral foam for silks and drieds
serrated knife
24" of 30-gauge wire
low temperature glue gun and sticks

1 Separate 20 strands of raffia from the bunch and set aside. Divide the remainder into two bunches and overlap one end of each bunch by 3". Wire the two bunches together at the overlap point, creating a 90" raffia garland. With the 20 strands, make a collar bow (see page 21) with two 5" loops and two 7" tails. Glue it to the center of the garland.

2 Cut the ribbon lengthwise into three pieces: two 5/8" wide lengths with a wired edge on one side and the center piece 1 1/2" wide with no wire. Cut the 1 1/2" wide piece into six 20" lengths and use each length to make a puffy bow (see page 20) with four 2 1/2" loops. Glue the bows 8 1/2", 24 1/2" and 40 1/2" to the right and left of the center raffia bow. Cut one 5/8" wide length into three 34" lengths and the other into two 34" and two 17" lengths. Wind each length around your finger to curl. Glue a 17" length under each end bow, extending down. Glue the 34" lengths from bow to bow, draped as shown in the large photo.

3 Glue a cluster of three apple slices to the garland at the center of the raffia bow and at each center point between the plaid bows. Cut 1/4 of the cedar into 1" sprigs. Glue three sprigs of cedar to the center of each apple cluster. Glue a 1" sprig of canella to the center of the cedar.

4 Trim a piece of foam to fit inside each tin container and glue to secure. Cut the German statice, remaining cedar and remaining canella into 1 1/2"–3" sprigs. Fill the tin containers with these sprigs, starting with the German statice and adding the cedar next. Conceal the foam with the moss, then glue the canella sprigs in place. Glue a container arrangement at the center of each plaid bow. Attach a wire hanger (see page 12) at the back of each container.

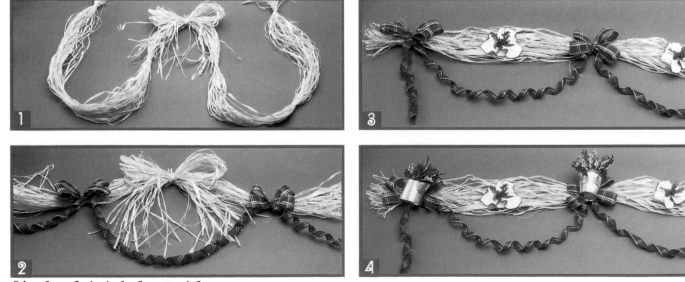

Garland with Naturals

5' green vinyl pine fireplace garland with a center cluster of twelve 3" long pine cones and a cluster of three 2" wide pine cones at each side
2 stems of orange/red latex bittersweet with a 10" and a 13" sprig of many ¼" wide berries and ¾" long leaves
four 3" long pine cones
six 1½"–2" wide dried pomegranates
eight 2" wide dried apple slices
nine 2"–3" wide dried orange slices
four 8" long cinnamon sticks
sixteen 4" long dried cinnamon sticks
10 oz. of dried barley
3 oz. of red dried small chili peppers
3 oz. of red dried canella
2 oz. of dried brisa media
6" of 24-gauge wire
low temperature glue gun and sticks

1 Glue two pine cones and a pomegranate near the right end and two near the left end of the garland. Glue two pomegranates among the center cones. Glue one on each side among the cones midway between the center and ends of the garland. Cut the wheat into 5" sprigs and wire together in clusters of five. Glue five clusters around the center pine cones, and one near each outer cone cluster. Glue three around each cone cluster between the center and garland ends.

2 Glue three apple slices among the center cone cluster. Glue one apple slice each near each remaining cone cluster. Glue three orange slices around the center pine cone cluster, two near each midway cluster and two near each outer cluster as shown.

3 Glue two 8" cinnamon sticks at the ends of the center cone cluster, extending as shown. Glue one 8" cinnamon stick between each of the the mid and outer clusters. Glue two 4" sticks near each mid and outer cluster; glue eight 4" sticks in pairs around the center cone cluster as shown. Cut the canella into 4" sprigs and glue evenly among the florals and greenery as shown.

4 Cut the bittersweet into two 10" and four 6½" sprigs. Glue a 10" sprig and a 6½" sprig at each end of the center fruit/cone cluster, extending as shown. Glue a 6½" sprig between each of the mid and outer clusters. Cut the brisa media into 6" sprigs and glue evenly among the florals and greenery.

52" green vinyl pine garland
2 stems of latex fruit, each with a 20" section of two 3" wide red/yellow apples, two 3" wide oranges, one 2½" wide green pear, one 3" wide green pear, two 2"–2½" plums, 1 cluster of five 1" wide red berries and 3 bunches of many ½" wide purple or green grapes
1 stem of latex fruit with a 2" wide peach, a 3" wide red apple, ¼" wide blue berries and a 2" long pine cone
1 holly bush with eleven 3" sprigs of five 2"–3" leaves and a cluster of ¼" wide red berries
1 stem of red berries with nine 6" branches of three to four 4" sprigs of many ¼" long berries
15 stems of 1" wide red dried roses
2 oz. of white preserved rice flower
3 oz. of dried black-bearded wheat
eleven 2" long pine cones
low temperature glue gun and sticks

Della Robbia Garland

1 Bend the garland into a gentle S-shape as shown. Bend each 20" fruit stem into a semi-circle. Wire one stem to each curve of the "S", leaving a 4" empty area at the center of the garland. Cut the stem off the small fruit stem and glue it at the center space.

2 Cut the holly into eleven 4" sprigs and glue among the fruit, alternating the sides. Cut the roses into 4" sprigs and glue singly or in pairs among the fruit as shown.

3 Cut the red berries into nine 6" sprigs and glue evenly spaced along the garland. Cut the rice flower into eight 3" long sprigs and glue as for the berries.

4 Glue the pine cones among the fruit, alternating from left to right. Cut the wheat into 5" sprigs and glue in loose clusters of three, evenly spaced throughout the garland.

Burnished Gold Festoon

9' green vinyl pine fireplace garland with eighteen
 1 ½"–3" long pine cones
3 ½ yards of 2 ½" wide burgundy/gold metallic tapestry
 ribbon with gold wired edges
3 stems of burgundy latex poinsettias, each with one 8"
 wide gold-glittered blossom

7 burgundy latex berry picks, each with two 1" long red
 berries, nine ½" wide gold-tipped red berries and
 four to five 2" long leaves
ten 3"–4" wide gold dried lotus pod picks
4 oz. of bronze preserved salal leaves
4 oz. of green preserved tree fern, lightly sprayed gold
12" of 24-gauge wire
low temperature glue gun and sticks

1 Bend the garland at a 90° angle, 27" from each end. Bend the center into a curve, then weave the ribbon among the pine along the entire length of the garland as shown. Attach a wire hanger (see page 12) to the back at each 90° bend.

2 Glue a lotus pod 5" to the right and the left of the center of the garland and another pod 10" from each end. Glue three near each 90° bend.

3 Cut the poinsettias into 4" sprigs. Glue one blossom at the center of the garland; glue one each 12" to the upper right and left of center. Cut the berry picks into 4" sprigs. Glue one 3" and one 6" to the left and to the right of the center poinsettia. Glue another sprig at each 90° bend and one 14" from each end.

4 Cut the salal into 4"–6" sprigs and glue evenly spaced among the greenery. Cut the tree fern into 7"–10" sprigs and glue among the greenery, extending toward the ends.

Triple Wheat Swag

6 oz. of 14" long dried wheat
5½ yards of ⅞" wide red/green/black plaid taffeta ribbon
3 gift picks, each with three ½" wide red gifts
2 oz. of green preserved Frasier fir
1 oz. of dried canella
12" of 24-gauge wire
low temperature glue gun and sticks

1 Divide the wheat into a 1½ oz., a 2 oz. and a 2½ oz. bunch. Wire each bunch together just below the wheat heads. Cut the ribbon into a 54", a 65" and a 77" length. Use the 54" length to make an oblong bow (see page 20) with a center loop, two 1½" loops, two 2½" loops and two 16" tails. Use the 65" length to make an oblong bow with a center loop, two 2" loops, four 2½" loops and two 16" tails. Use the 77" length to make an oblong bow with a center loop, two 2" loops, four 2½" loops, two 3" loops and two 16" tails.

2 Wire the first bow to the front of the smallest wheat bunch at the wiring point. Repeat with the second bow on the medium wheat bunch and the last bow on the largest bunch. Wrap the tails of each bow to the back, cross, then back around to the front as shown. On the third wrap, glue the tails to the back to secure and trim any excess ribbon.

3 Wire the stalk end of the small wheat bunch under the heads of the medium bunch as shown. Trim excess stems from the small bunch. Wire the medium bunch to the large bunch in the same manner so that all three bunches are wired together as shown.

4 Cut the fir into 1"–3" sprigs and glue evenly spaced around each bow. Cut the canella into 1" sprigs and glue three sprigs around the center loop of each bow. Cut the gifts off the picks and glue as for the canella. Attach a wire hanger (see page 12) at the top back.

Country Swag

30" green vinyl pine door swag with many 8"–10" sprigs

3 ½ yards of 2 ½" wide red/tan checked ribbon with soldiers

4 stems of red latex raspberries, each with two 4" long sprigs of five ½" wide berries and many 1 ½" long leaves

1 stem of green/burgundy silk maple leaves with twenty-two 1"–2" long leaves

4 oz. of green preserved cedar

2 oz. of dried avena

3 oz. of dried papaver

2 oz. of dried twigs

eight 3"–4" long pine cones

12" of 24-gauge wire

low temperature glue gun and sticks

1 Cut the cedar into 6" sprigs and glue evenly among the pine, extending downward. Use the ribbon to make an oblong bow (see page 20) with a center loop, four 3" loops, six 5" loops and two 16" tails. Glue the bow to the center top of the swag with the tails extending downward.

2 Cut the raspberry stems into eight sprigs, each with five berries. Glue a sprig to the right and one left of the bow, both extending downward. Glue the remaining sprigs evenly spaced among the greenery as shown. Cut the maple leaves into 5" sprigs of 2–3 leaves and glue evenly spaced among the greenery.

3 Cut the avena into 5" sprigs and glue evenly spaced among the greenery in clusters of 3–4. Glue the pine cones evenly spaced among the greenery angled toward the sides and bottom.

4 Cut the twigs into 10" sprigs and glue evenly among the greens, extending outward around the bow and downward among the pine sprigs. Cut the papaver into 4" sprigs; glue in clusters of three evenly spaced among the greenery as shown. Attach a wire hanger (see page 12) at the top back.

32"x12" TWIGS™ wall plaque
3 ⅓ yards of ¼" wide red velvet cord
2 stems of green vinyl pine, each with twenty-eight 5" sprigs
1 stem of red silk poinsettias with three 6" wide and two 4" wide blossoms
1 stem of green silk holly with six sprigs of six 2" long leaves and 1 cluster of three ¼" wide red berries
eight 1"–1 ¾" wide brown cone flowers
2 oz. of white preserved rice flower
3 oz. of dried bromus secalinus
12" of 24-gauge wire
low temperature glue gun and sticks

Victorian Poinsettia Swag

1 Cut the pine branches into 5" sprigs and glue across the bottom of the plaque, extending as shown.

2 Cut the poinsettias into five 2" sprigs. Glue a 6" blossom at the left end, one at the right end and one at the center. Glue the 4" blossoms in the spaces between. Cut the holly into six 2" sprigs. Glue evenly spaced among the greenery, alternating placement from top to bottom.

3 Glue the cone flowers evenly spaced among the greenery as for the holly. Cut the rice flower into eleven 3" long sprigs and glue evenly spaced among the greenery.

4 Cut the bromus into 5" sprigs and glue in clusters of 3–6 stems evenly spaced as shown. Use the cord to make a shoestring bow (see page 18) with 4" loops and 6½" tails. Glue it at the center bottom of the plaque. With the remaining cord, cut one 24", one 28" and one 34" length. Drape from the bottom of the crown and glue at each end. Glue the center of each length at the center of the swag, behind the bow, to create loops as shown in large photo. Attach a wire hanger (see page 12) at the top back.

Poinsettia Window Valance

36" wide TWIGS™ swag
3 stems of white latex poinsettias, each with a 6" wide blossom
   and a sprig with one 1½" wide orange apple, three 1" wide purple berries and seven 2"–5" long leaves
2 stems of purple latex grapes, each with three 3"–4" long clusters
   of many ½" wide grapes
five 2"–3" long flocked pine cones
2 oz. of white preserved ti-tree
4 oz. of green preserved spruce
4 oz. of green preserved spiral eucalyptus
two 1" metal curtain hooks
low temperature glue gun and sticks

4 Cut the ti-tree into 4"–6" sprigs and the spruce into 5" sprigs; glue them evenly spaced among the florals, extending as for the eucalyptus. Glue the curtain hooks to the back center of the swag, 15" apart. Hang the swag on a standard curtain rod. Wire hangers (see page 12) can be substituted for the curtain hooks if the swag is to be hung on a wall.

1 Cut the eucalyptus into 3"–6" sprigs. Glue across the middle 30" of the swag, extending as shown.

2 Glue the poinsettias evenly spaced across the middle of the swag. Extend the fruit stems of the two outer blossoms toward the swag ends. Extend the fruit stem of the center blossom to the left.

3 Cut the grapes into six 4" sprigs and glue evenly spaced among the florals. Glue the pine cones as shown in the large photo above.

Gilded Poinsettia Swag

30" long green vinyl pine door swag with many 3"–10" pine sprigs and seven 3"–5" long pine cones

3⅓ yards of 2½" wide burgundy/gold brocade ribbon with gold wired edges

1 stem of white latex poinsettias with one 8" and one 6" wide blossom, two ¾"–2" wide orange/red pomegranates, one 1½" burgundy apple, one 1" wide green apple, two 1"–1½" wide red raspberries, one ¾" wide cherry and many 4" long leaves

1 stem of white latex poinsettias with one 7" blossom, one 1¼" wide gold apple, two ½" wide cherries, three ½"–1" wide raspberries, and many 4" leaves

2 stems of purple latex grapes, each with three 3" long clusters of many ½" grapes

3 oz. of brown preserved eucalyptus

three 3" wide dried lotus pods

3 oz. of red dried amaranthus

2 oz. of dried twigs

2 oz. of dried bromus grass, sprayed gold

12" of 24-gauge wire

low temperature glue gun and sticks

1 Cut the poinsettia stem with two large blossoms to 14" long and glue to the swag with the stem end at the center top of the swag. Cut the remaining poinsettia stem to 10" and glue it under the double poinsettia stem, extending down. Cut the eucalyptus into 6" sprigs and glue evenly among the greenery, extending downward.

2 Cut the grape stems into six 4" sprigs and glue evenly spaced among the greenery, on either side of the poinsettias. Cut the twigs into 8" sprigs and glue evenly among the floral and greenery area.

3 Cut the gold bromus grass into 6" sprigs and glue evenly spaced among the florals and greenery. Cut the lotus pod stems to 3" and glue one to the upper right of the top poinsettia, one to the lower left of the middle poinsettia and one centered 4" below the lowest poinsettia.

4 With the ribbon, make an oblong bow (see page 20) with a center loop, two 3" loops, six 5" loops and four 9" tails. Glue to the center top of the swag. Cut the amaranthus into 5" sprigs and glue evenly among the florals and greenery. Attach a wire hanger (see page 12) at the top back.

Door Bouquet

8 oz. of 30" long dried maple twigs
1 ¾ yards of 4" wide burgundy twisted paper ribbon
two 2" long peach/brown mushroom birds
one 3" wide twig bird nest
6 oz. of green preserved Frasier fir
4 oz. of dried bell reed
4 oz. of white preserved ti-tree
2 oz. of green preserved salal leaves
1 oz. of green dried sphagnum moss
six 2" long pine cones
4"x4"x2" block of floral foam for silks and drieds
serrated knife
6" of 24-gauge wire
one floral U-pin
low temperature glue gun and sticks

1 Cut the twigs into 7"–15" branches and glue into one side of the foam block, the shorter branches toward the sides and the longer ones in the center. Cut twelve 5" sprigs from the leftover ends and glue into the opposite side of the foam as shown. Glue moss around the sides of the foam.

2 Cut the bell reed into 6"–10" sprigs and glue in front of and among the branches as shown. Cut the Frasier fir into 5"–8" sprigs; glue and insert to cover the foam, angling all the sprigs toward the long branches and with the shorter sprigs on the sides extending slightly outward. Cut the salal into 4" sprigs and glue evenly spaced among the greenery.

3 Cut six 10" lengths of ribbon and make a ribbon loop (see page 21) with each. Glue the loops among the lower greenery as shown. Glue the bird nest to the fir slightly above and right of the center. Glue one bird into the nest and one to the left of the nest.

4 Glue three pine cones just above the bird nest. Glue the remaining cones among the loops. Cut the ti-tree into 5"–7" sprigs and glue evenly among the greenery, extending in similar directions. Glue a U-pin for a hanger at the upper back of the foam.

Vertical Swag

1 1/4" x 18" x 1/4" wood strip
2 1/4 yards of 2 5/8" wide green ribbon with wired edges
3 stems of red latex poinsettias, each with one 4"–4 1/2" wide blossom, four 1/2" wide berries and three 2" long flocked pine sprigs
1 stem of gold silk roses with three 1" wide blossoms, two 1/2" wide buds and three 1"–2" long leaves, lightly sprayed with gold glitter
2 stems of red latex berries, each with three 3" long clusters of 1/4" wide berries
four 1 1/2" long pine cones
2 oz. of white preserved heather
6 oz. of green preserved cedar
4 oz. of gray American Moss™
gold spray glitter
12" of 24-gauge wire
low temperature glue gun and sticks

1 Wrap the wooden strip completely in American Moss and glue to secure. Cut the cedar into 4 1/2" sprigs. Starting at the bottom, glue the sprigs to the wrapped strip with the sprigs extending downward on both sides as shown.

2 Cut the poinsettias to 2" sprigs and glue among the greenery as shown. Cut the gold roses and buds into four 2" sprigs and glue them and the pine cones evenly spaced among the greenery.

3 Cut the berries into six 3" sprigs and glue to the swag extending downward alternating from side to side. Cut the heather into 4" sprigs and glue evenly spaced among the greenery.

4 Use the ribbon to make an oblong bow (see page 20) with a center loop, two 4" loops, four 5" loops and two 10" tails. Glue the bow to the center top of the swag as shown. Attach a wire hanger (see page 12) at the top back of the swag.

CHRISTMAS CARD holder

5 yards of 3½" wide red/green/blue holiday print ribbon with wired
   edges
1 stem of red silk poppies with five 2" wide blossoms
1 stem of white silk baby's breath with three 3" long clusters of many
   ¼" wide blossoms
1 stem of green silk holly with 3 clusters of four to six ¼"–⅜" wide
   red berries and many leaves
two 3" long pine cones
1 floral U-pin
12" of 24-gauge wire
low temperature glue gun and sticks

1 Cut a 40" and a 56" length of ribbon. Use the remaining
ribbon to make a puffy bow (see page 20) with six 6" loops
and two 6" tails. Set the bow aside for step 2. The 40" length
will be the backing for the holder and the 56" length will form
the pockets. Place the 40" length face upon the table. Fold one
end of the 56" length under and glue 2" from the lower end of
the 40" piece. Measure 8" up the 56" length and glue it to the
40" ribbon at this point (this forms the lowest card pocket).
Measure another 8" up the longest length; this time glue it 6"
away from the first glued spot on the 40" length. Continue up
the two lengths forming a total of five pockets. Cut an inverted
"V" at the bottom of the 40" length.

2 Glue the bow to the five-pocket ribbon so that the bottom
of the bow is at the top of the upper pocket. Glue the U-pin

to the upper back for a hanger. Cut the cedar into
5" sprigs and glue evenly spaced among the bow
loops as shown.

3 Cut the holly into three 4" sprigs of berries
and leaves and two sprigs of two leaves. Glue
evenly spaced among the bow loops. Glue the pine
cones to the center of the bow as shown.

4 Cut the poppies into five 2" sprigs and glue to
the bow with one at the right and left of the
pine cones, one under the lower cone and two above
the upper cone. Cut the baby's breath into nine 1"
sprigs. Glue them evenly spaced among the florals
and greenery.

Grapes and Roses Swag

30" long green vinyl pine door swag with many 3"–10"
  long pine sprigs and seven 3"–5" long pine cones
5 yards of 2½" wide burgundy/green/gold tapestry ribbon
  with wired edges
5 stems of ivory latex roses, each with one 4½" wide
  blossom and 2 clusters of five 2" long leaves
2 stems of purple latex grapes, each with three 3"–4" long
  clusters of many ⅜"–⅝" wide grapes
2 stems of white silk heather, each with three 7" long
  sprigs of many branched blossoms
2 stems of white silk vervain, each with three 7" long
  sprigs of green white-tipped blossoms
3 oz. of burgundy dried hillflowers
12" of 24-gauge wire
low temperature glue gun and sticks

1 Cut the roses into five 4" sprigs and the rose leaf
clusters into ten 4" sprigs. Glue the roses among
the pine branches as shown; glue a sprig of leaves on
each side of each rose.

2 Cut the grapes into six 4" sprigs and glue one to
the left of the upper left blossom and to the right
the upper right blossom. Glue the remaining grape
sprigs down the swag, alternating from side to side as
shown. Cut the heather into six 7" sprigs and glue
among the greenery as shown.

3 Use the ribbon to make an oblong bow (see page
20) with a center loop, two 5" loops, two 5½"
loops, two 6" loops, two 7" loops, two 8½" loops, one
18" tail and one 26" tail. Glue the bow at the top of
the swag over the large pine cone and arrange the
tails as shown.

4 Cut the hillflowers into 5" sprigs and glue in clusters of 6–8, evenly spaced among the greenery.
Cut the vervain into six 7" sprigs and glue among the
greenery as shown. Attach a wire hanger (see page 12)
at the top back of the swag.

Christmas Arch

one 9"x32" TWIGS™ wall plaque
3 yards of 1½" wide gold white herringbone print ribbon
1 stem of white silk roses with three 2" wide blossoms, one 1¼" wide bud and six 2" long leaves
1 stem of white silk plum blossoms with seven 4½" sprigs of one to five 1" blossoms and many 2" leaves
1 stem of green silk holly with five 4" wide sprigs of five 1"–3" leaves and a cluster of ¼" red berries
4 oz. of green preserved cedar
two 3" long flocked pine cones
12" of 24-gauge wire
low temperature glue gun and sticks

1 Use the ribbon to make two standup bows (see page 19), each with a 3" loop, a 4" loop, a 6" loop, one 6" tail and one 16" tail. Make an additional 4" loop (see page 19). Glue the bows with the tails draped across the arch and glue as shown. Glue the single loop between the loops of the other bows, extending upward.

2 Cut the cedar into 4"–6" sprigs and glue among the bow loops and tails as shown. Cut a large rose into a 2" sprigs; glue it to the center of the plaque. Cut the rest of the rose stems into four 3" sprigs with a large blossom or bud. Glue a 2" blossom 3½" to the right and one to the left of the center rose. Glue the buds to the lower left and upper right of the center rose, extending as shown.

3 Cut the holly into five 4" sprigs. Glue one between the center and left bow loops. Glue one to the lower left and one to the right of the center rose. Glue one beyond the outer rose on each side.

4 Cut the plum blossom stem into seven 4½" sprigs and glue them evenly spaced among the cedar and among the bow loops. Glue a pine cone to the upper left and one to the lower right of the center rose as shown.

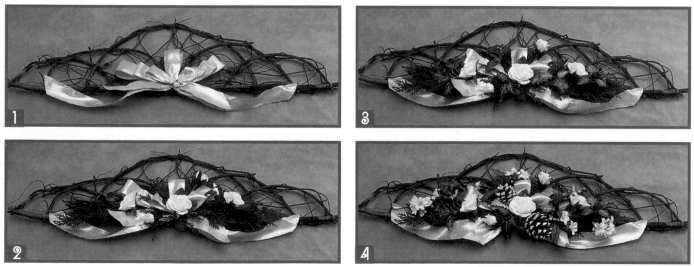

Country Christmas Bird Cage

7"x6½"x22" twig bird cage

2½ yards of 2½" wide red/tan checked ribbon with wired edges

one 40" long green vinyl pine garland

1 green silk holly bush with nine 3" sprigs, each with six 1½"–3" long leaves and 1 cluster of ¼" wide berries

2 stems of cream silk statice, each with three 4" sprigs, one 3" sprig and one 1" sprig of many ¾" wide blossoms

3 oz. of red preserved tree fern

3 oz. of white dried floral buttons

eight 1" long pine cones

2 oz. of dried birch twigs

two 3" long green/brown mushroom birds

12" of 24-gauge wire

low temperature glue gun and sticks

1 Glue one end of the pine garland at the top of the bird cage, near the hanger and drape it down the left side. At 6" from the bottom, push the garland through the bars of the bird cage and then pull it through the right side. Use the ribbon to make an oblong bow (see page 20) with a center loop, two 4½" loops, two 6" loops and one 40" tail. Glue the bow at the top right of the bird cage and drape the tail through the greenery as shown.

2 Cut the holly into nine 3" sprigs, the statice into eight 4" sprigs; glue the two smaller statice sprigs together to form a large cluster. Glue the statice and holly sprigs evenly spaced along the garland.

3 Cut the tree fern into 4" sprigs and glue evenly spaced among the other materials, extending downward. Cut the floral buttons into 4" sprigs and glue in clusters of 7–9 throughout the greenery, angling downward left and right.

4 Glue one bird at the left of the bird cage roof and the other bird at the lower right where the garland emerges through the bars. Glue the pine cones along the length of the garland, angling from left and right as shown. Cut the birch twigs into 7"–9" sprigs and glue among the greenery, extending downward.

Country Christmas Wreath

18" crossed twig wreath
1 ⅓ yards of 2½" wide red/tan checked
    ribbon with wired edges
one 36" long green vinyl pine garland
1 stem of green silk holly with nine 2"
    long sprigs, each with six 1½"–3"
    long leaves and 1 cluster of ¼" wide
    berries
1 stem of cream silk statice with three 4"
    sprigs, one 3" sprig and one 1" sprig
    of many ¾" wide blossoms

2 oz. of red preserved tree fern
2 oz. of white dried floral buttons
seven 1" long pine cones
one 2½" long tan/white mushroom bird
one 3" wide brown fiber bird nest
12" of 24-gauge wire
low temperature glue gun and sticks

1 Bend the garland into a circle and wire it to the wreath with the sprigs extending clockwise. Use the ribbon to make an oblong bow (see page 20) with a center loop, two 3" loops, two 4" loops and two 8" tails. Glue the bow at the top of the wreath and glue the tails at 3:00 and 9:00. Attach a wire hanger (see page 12) to the top back of the wreath.

2 Cut the holly into nine 3" sprigs and the statice into five 4" sprigs; glue the two smaller statice sprigs together to form a large cluster. Glue the holly and statice sprigs evenly among the greenery.

3 Cut the tree fern into 4" sprigs and glue evenly spaced, extending clockwise among the florals. Cut the floral buttons into 4" sprigs and glue in clusters of 6 evenly spaced around the wreath.

4 Glue one pine cone below the bow center and the rest evenly spaced around the wreath. Glue the bird nest to the inside bottom of the wreath, then glue the bird into the nest.

Berry Bounty Wreath

12" wide grapevine wreath

2¾ yards of 2½" wide green/burgundy/black partridge-in-a-pear-tree printed ribbon

one 45" long green vinyl pine garland with eight 2"–2½" long pine cones

1 stem of yellow latex raspberries with four 6" long sprigs of two or three ½"–¾" wide berries and three to five 2"–3" long green leaves

three 2" wide dried pomegranates

five 2" wide dried apple slices

five 2"–2½" wide dried orange slices

3 oz. of red dried pepper berries

2 oz. of dried silene grass

12" of 24-gauge wire

low temperature glue gun and sticks

1 Wire the garland to the wreath clockwise, leaving a 13" tail extending to the right as shown. Use the ribbon to make an oblong bow (see page 20) with a center loop, two 3½" loops, two 4" loops, two 5" loops, one 17" tail and one 22" tail. Trim the tails diagonally. Glue the bow just above the greenery tail, angled as shown. Weave the 17" tail among the greenery of the tail and glue to secure. Weave the 22" tail up the left side of the wreath and glue to secure.

2 Glue three orange slices to the wreath, evenly spaced among the greenery and two slices to the tail. Glue three apple slices to the wreath and two slices to the tail as shown.

3 Glue the pomegranates to the wreath, one at 1:00, one at 5:00 to the left of the bow and one at 10:00. Cut the raspberries into four 6" sprigs, then cut one of the sprigs with three berries into a 2-berry and 1-berry sprig. Glue the three large sprigs on the wreath and the two small sprigs on the tail, all evenly spaced as shown.

4 Cut the pepper berries into 1½"–3" sprigs and glue evenly spaced among the greenery. Cut the silene grass into 4" sprigs and glue clockwise around the wreath, evenly spaced and alternating from inside to outside. Attach a wire hanger (see page 12) at the top back.

Berry Bounty Garland

60" green vinyl pine garland with thirteen 2" long pine cones

5¼ yards of 2⅝" wide green/burgundy/black partridge-in-a-pear-tree printed ribbon

1 stem of yellow latex raspberries with four 6" long sprigs of two to three ¾" wide berries and three to five 2½"–3½" long green leaves

five 2" wide dried pomegranates

seven 2"–2½" wide dried apple slices

six 2½" wide dried orange slices

4 oz. of red dried pepper berries

3 oz. of dried silene grass

6" of 24-gauge wire

low temperature glue gun and sticks

1 Bend the garland 90° at points 16" from each end and attach wire hangers (see page 12) at the back of each bend. Use the ribbon to make two oblong bows (see page 20), each with a center loop, two 4" loops, two 4½" loops, two 5" loops and two 17" tails. Trim the tails diagonally. Glue one bow at each bend and weave the tails among the pine as shown. Glue the tail ends to secure.

2 Glue one apple slice above each bow and the rest evenly spaced among the greenery. Glue the orange slices evenly spaced among the greenery as shown in the large photo.

3 Glue the pomegranates among the greenery with three across the top and one near each end. Cut the raspberries into four 5" sprigs and glue among the greenery.

4 Cut the pepper berries into 2"–4" sprigs and glue evenly spaced among the pine sprigs. Cut the silene grass into 4" sprigs and glue among the pine sprigs, with the sprigs across the top extending to the right and the sprigs on the sides extending downward as shown.

fruit Centerpiece Trio

FOR THE MIDDLE SECTION:
32" green vinyl pine garland
1 stem of green latex holly with four 5" sprigs, each
   with 1 cluster of four to six ½" wide berries and five
   2"–3" long leaves
2 latex fruit picks, each with one 4" long pear, one 2"
   wide pomegranate, one 3" long pine cone, 2
   clusters of three ½" wide blueberries and five 2"–4"
   long leaves

2 stems of red latex frosted berries, each with three 3"
   long clusters of many ½"–⅝" wide red berries
2 oz. of dried black-bearded wheat
2 oz. of white dried bloom broom
four 2"–2½" wide red latex apples
four 4" long pine cones, painted red and flocked
three 1" wide candle cups, three 12" tall taper candles
24" of 24-gauge wire
low temperature glue gun and sticks

1 Cut the garland in half and wire together to make a 30" piece. Fluff the
pine branches so the garland lays flat. Glue one candle cup in the center
and one 8" away on each side. Glue a large fruit pick on each side of the center candle cup, extending as shown.

2 Glue one flocked pine cone at each end of the garland and two in the
center, angled as shown. Glue the apples evenly spaced as shown.

3 Cut the frosted berries into six 4" sprigs and glue evenly spaced extending
from the center toward the ends. Cut the wheat into 4" sprigs and glue a
cluster of three sprigs by each frosted berry sprig.

4 Cut the holly into
four 5" sprigs. Glue
one sprig on each side of
the flocked pine cones at
the ends of the garland.
Cut the bloom broom
into 4" sprigs and glue
evenly spaced among the
greenery. Insert a candle
into each candle cup.

FOR THE END SECTIONS:
70" green vinyl pine garland with two 2"
   long pine cones
2 stems of green latex holly, each with
   four 5" sprigs of 1 cluster of four to six
   ½" wide berries and five 2"–3" long
   leaves

2 latex fruit picks, each with one 4" long pear,
   one 2" wide pomegranate, one 3" long pine
   cone, 2 clusters of three ½" wide blueberries
   and five 2"–4" long leaves
2 stems of red latex frosted berries, each with
   three 3" long clusters of many ½"–⅝" wide
   red berries
2 oz. of dried black-bearded wheat
2 oz. of white dried bloom broom

four 4" long pine cones, painted red and flocked
four 2" wide red latex apples
low temperature glue gun and sticks

5 Cut the garland in half; bend each half into a semicircle. Cut the latex fruit picks apart and glue the fruit, leaves, berries and pine cone from one pick in the center area of each half as shown.

6 Glue the flocked pine cones to each half, one at 3" from the right end and one 7" from the left end. Glue two latex apples to each half, one at the center and one at the left end.

7 Cut the frosted berries into six 4" sprigs and glue three to each half, one at the center and one at each end. Cut the wheat into 4" sprigs; glue six clusters of three stems each to each half, evenly spaced and extending from the center toward the ends.

8 Cut the holly into eight 5" sprigs and glue four onto each half, evenly spaced among the greenery. Cut the bloom broom into 4" sprigs and glue evenly spaced among the greenery on both half.

Treasured Trims for the Tree

Floral materials can be very effectively used when creating Christmas tree decorations. And they look wonderful when displayed, adding color, texture and warmth as well as reinforcing the festive atmosphere created by the tree.

Silk and dried flowers are perfect enhancements for the tree, especially if a woodsy or natural feeling is needed. For a back-to-nature look, create the more rustic designs such as the Vine Ball on page 110 and the birdhouse and pine cone ornaments on page 108. Then add bouquets of baby's breath, wheat, twigs, all tied together with raffia, among the tree branches. Paper ribbon bows can be wired onto the ends of the branches and will provide color as well as texture and interest to the whole tree.

To add a bit of shine to the tree, include white twinkling lights among the branches. If a bit more glitz is desired, add some satin glass balls among the natural ornaments.

Florals also provide the finishing touches to a Victorian tree. roses clustered with baby's breath can be tied onto branches with ribbon or cording. Or, create tussie mussies by clustering several different flowers and tucking them into a cone formed from a doily.

Also included here are two pages of ideas for creatively wrapping gifts to go under the tree. This reinforces the look and feeling established by the tree ornaments. Many times the bow enhancement shown can be adapted to be an ornament just by adding a hanger to it. As with the ornaments, these package decorations are quick, easy, inexpensive and fun for the whole family to make.

Christmas Star & Small Swag

5" wide papier maché star ornament
⅓ yard of ⅞" wide green variegated ribbon with wired edges
1 stem of dark pink silk roses with three ¾" wide blossoms
6 stems of dried bromus secalinus
1 stem of dried rice flower with a 2" wide head
6" of 24-gauge wire
low temperature glue gun and sticks

1 Use the ribbon to make a shoestring bow (see page 18) with two 2" loops and two 2" tails. Glue the bow to the center of the star. Cut the bromus secalinus into 2" sprigs and glue the ends of the sprigs to the center of the bow.

2 Cut the roses into three 1" sprigs and glue in a triangular cluster at the bow center. Cut the rice flower into three 1" sprigs and glue evenly spaced around the roses. Crinkle the ribbon tails.

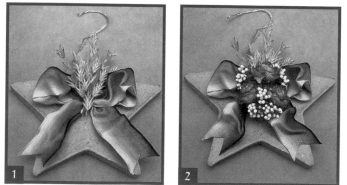

one ¾"x6" long wood craft stick
½ yard of 1½" wide green/gold/red poinsettia print ribbon
6" of ⅛" wide green satin ribbon
1 oz. of green preserved cedar
¼ oz. of white dried caspia
1 red berry pick with six 1½" long sprigs of six ⅛" berries
⅜ yard of 1mm gold fused beads
6" of 24-gauge
low temperature glue gun and sticks

1 Form a 4" green ribbon loop and attach it to the top back of the craft stick to form a hanger. Cut the cedar into 2½" sprigs and glue to the stick angled outward as shown.

2 Use the 1½" ribbon to make an oblong bow (see page 20) with two 1½" loops and two 2" loops. Glue it at the top of the swag. Cut the red berries into 2" sprigs and glue evenly spaced extending downward as shown. Glue one end of the bead garland at the top back of the swag. Wrap the garland three times down the swag with 1½" between wraps, then glue at the lower back. Cut the caspia into 1" sprigs and glue evenly spaced as for the berries.

Victorian Floral Ball & Cinnamon and Lace

one 3" gold plastic ball ornament
one 8" round white crocheted doily with ivory edges
⅔ yard of ¼" wide white satin ribbon
2 stems of white silk roses, each with three 1" blossoms
¼ oz. of green preserved plumosus fern
¼ oz. of burgundy preserved leptospurnum
low temperature glue gun and sticks

1   Cut a 12" length of ribbon and weave it
    through the doily 1" from the edges. Slip the
center of the doily over the loop on the ornament
ball. Pull the ribbon tightly to fit the doily to the
ball and tie in a shoestring bow with two 1" loops
and two 1" tails. Thread the remaining ribbon
through the ornament loop and knot the ends to
form a hanger.

2   Cut the roses off the stems and glue them
    evenly spaced around the top of the ornament.
Cut the plumosus into 1" sprigs. Glue two sprigs to
the bow at the bottom of the ornament. Glue the
remaining sprigs evenly spaced among the rose
blossoms. Cut the leptospurnum into 1"–2" sprigs;
glue two sprigs to the bow and the rest evenly
among the roses as shown.

five 5" long cinnamon sticks
⅓ yard of ⅛" wide lavender satin ribbon
one 4" round white crocheted doily
one 1" wide mauve silk rose blossom
five 1"– 3" stems of green preserved plumosus fern
two 1½" long stems of lavender dried Siberian statice
6" of 24-gauge wire
low temperature glue gun and sticks

1   Use the wire to fasten the cinnamon sticks in a
    bundle. Wrap the doily around the cinnamon
bundle. Secure the doily by threading the ribbon
through both sides of the doily. Align the ribbon
ends and knot tightly against the cinnamon bundle.
Knot the ends of ribbon to form hanger.

2   Glue the rose blossom to the doily at the top
    center as shown. Glue the plumosus around
the rose with the longer sprigs extending toward
the ends. Repeat with the Siberian statice.

Mini Birdhouse & Iced Pine Cone

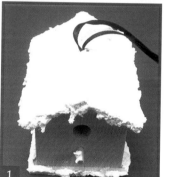

2"x 2½"x2¼" wooden birdhouse
9" of ⅛" wide green satin ribbon
one 5" long branch of blueberry juniper
one 5" long sprig of dark red glittered German statice
two ¾" long mini yellow/brown mushroom birds
decorative textured "snow" paint
low temperature glue gun and sticks.

1 Fold the ribbon in half and knot the ends. Glue the knot at the center of the roof. Generously coat the roof (covering the ribbon knot), base and perch of the birdhouse with the snow paint; leave a rough texture and allow it to hang over the edges like icicles. Let dry.

2 Cut the juniper and German statice into 1" sprigs and glue evenly spaced around the bird-house base. Glue six 1" sprigs of juniper and four 1" sprigs of German statice to the roof with the stem ends together as shown. Glue one bird over the stem ends and the other bird on the perch.

5" long pine cone
¼ yard of ¼" wide white satin ribbon
three 4" sprigs of green vinyl pine
three 2" long frosted/glittered green silk ivy leaves
1 raspberry pick with twelve ½" wide red berries
6" of 24-gauge wire
spray snow
low temperature glue gun and sticks

1 Spray the pine cone and the pine evenly with the spray snow and let dry. Fold the ribbon in half and wire or glue the ends to the base of the cone as shown to form a hanger. Glue the pine sprigs evenly spaced around the hanger and bend them to extend over the sides of the cone as shown.

2 Glue the ivy leaves evenly spaced among the pine sprigs. Cut the binding from the berry pick. Cut the berries into 1" sprigs and glue them evenly among the pine and ivy.

Lacy Heart & Country Basket

one 3" long wood heart cutout with ⅛" hole at the center top
one 3½" white battenburg heart
1 burgundy rose pick with a 1" wide blossom and two ¾" long buds
one 6" sprig of green preserved cedar
⅛ oz. of white glittered, preserved baby's breath
1 yard of ⅛" wide green satin ribbon
low temperature glue gun and sticks

1 Cut an 8" length of ribbon and insert it through the hole in the center top of the heart. Knot the ends together to form a hanger. Weave the remaining ribbon through the outside edge of the lace heart as shown, tying the ends into a shoestring bow (see page 18) with 1½" loops and 3" tails. Glue the doily centered over the wooden heart.

2 Glue the large rose at the center top of the heart. Glue a rosebud to the right and one to the left of the large rose. Cut the cedar into 1" sprigs and glue around the roses in an arch as shown. Cut the baby's breath into ½"–1" sprigs and glue evenly among the cedar sprigs.

one 1½"x3"x2" wood basket with a 1½" tall handle
6" of ⅛" white satin ribbon
1 berry pick with three 1" wide clusters of ⅛" red berries
½ oz. of green preserved cedar
¼ oz. of white dried German statice
three 1" long mini pine cones, sprayed gold
1½"x 3"x2" piece of floral foam for silks and drieds
serrated knife
low temperature glue gun and sticks

1 Glue the foam into the basket. Cut the cedar into 1½" sprigs and glue the stems into the foam with the sprigs extending over the outside edge of the basket.

2 Cut the German statice into 1½" sprigs and the berry pick into three 2" sprigs and glue evenly spaced among the cedar. Glue the pine cones as shown. Knot the ribbon in a loop around the handle to form a hanger. Glue the knot under the handle.

Rustic Vine Ball

one 4" wide woven vine
  ball
1 ¼ yards ¼" wide
  green/burgundy print
  ribbon
4 burgundy latex berry
  picks, each with three
  3" long sprigs of three
  to six ⅛" round
  berries
½ oz. of green pre-
  served ming fern
eight 1" long pine cones
1 oz. of green preserved
  cedar
1 oz. of dried caspia
low temperature glue
  gun and sticks

1 Cut a 7" length of ribbon, fold in half and glue it to the top of the ball
to form a hanger. Cut three 5" lengths of ribbon, fold in half and glue
these loops evenly spaced around the hanger. Cut three 7" lengths and glue
one end of each between the loops. Twist the free ends twice to form two
cascading tails and glue to the side of the ball.

2 Cut the ming fern into 2"–3" sprigs and glue to extend from under the
loops and tails down the vine ball as shown. Glue the pine cones to the
vine ball, with one on each side of the hanger loop and the rest spaced
among the fern.

3 Cut the cedar into 1"–2" sprigs and glue evenly spaced among the fern
and pine cones, angled downward. Cut the caspia into 1"–2½" sprigs
and glue among the
other materials, extend-
ing downward.

4 Cut the red berries
into twelve 3" sprigs
and glue evenly spaced
among the other materi-
als, extending downward
as shown.

Cardinal with Barley Swag & Cardinal in a Nest

½ yard of ⅛" wide green satin ribbon
1 holiday pick with a 1" red apple, two ½" apple slices and five ½"–1½" green/white holly leaves
one 2"x4" red mushroom cardinal
1½ oz. of dried barley
9" of 20-gauge wire
low temperature glue gun and sticks

1 Trim the barley to 7" and divide it into two bunches. Overlap the stems of the bunches and wire together to form a 9" swag as shown. Knot the ribbon tightly in the center of the swag. Allow the ribbon ends to hang down to be used when attaching the ornament to the tree.

2 Cut the stem on the holiday pick to ½" and glue it across the barley ends so the fruit is positioned just left of the swag center. Glue the cardinal to the right of the swag center, behind the pick.

4"x2" round twig nest
1 oz. of green preserved cedar
¼ oz. of white dried German statice
¼ oz. of red dried pepper berries
¼ oz. of green dried spagnum moss
9" of 20-gauge wire
low temperature glue gun and sticks

1 Glue the moss into the nest. Glue the cardinal to the front center of the nest. Cut the cedar into 4" sprigs. Glue two sprigs directly behind the cardinal extending upward and the remaining cedar extending over the edges of the nest as shown.

2 Cut the German statice into 3"–4" sprigs; glue the sprigs evenly around the cardinal. Glue the pepper berries to the front of the nest extending over the edge on each side of the cardinal. Insert one end of the piece of wire into the bottom center of the nest and push back down again. Leave the ends hanging down to attach the ornament to the tree.

Rolled Foam Ornaments

Styrofoam® balls: three 2" wide and one 3" wide
9" of each satin ribbon: 1/8" wide white, 1/8" wide green and 1/4" wide white
9" of gold metallic cord
1/2 oz. dried materials: lavender, potpourri, larkspur and crumbled wheat stalks
8" of 24-gauge wire
tacky craft glue

1 Cut a 2" piece of wire and fold it in half like a hairpin. Fold the ribbon or cord in half, insert the wire through the ends, dip the wire in glue and insert the wire into the ball. Repeat for each ball, using the 1/4" wide white satin ribbon for the largest ball.

2 Break or crumble the dried materials to 1/4" or smaller so they will lay smoothly against the surface of the ball.

3 Slide the knotted ribbon down to the wire. Apply glue thickly to the entire surface of the ball. Be sure to cover the loose ends of the ribbon or cord but not the wire hanger.

4 Holding the ball by the loop, roll it several times in the dried material. Refer to the large photo to match appropriate hangers and materials; note the largest ball is rolled in lavender. Fill any uncovered areas by pinching the materials between your fingers and pushing them into the glue. Let dry.

Tree Bow

2 yards of 3" wide burgundy sheer ribbon with gold wired edges
1 stem of gold silk roses with one 6" sprig of three 1½" wide blossoms, two ½" wide buds and nine 1½" long gold-glittered green leaves
1 stem of red latex berries with five 1½" long sprigs of three ½" wide berries
1 cone pick with six 2" long sprigs of two ½" long flocked pine cones
9" of 24–gauge wire
low temperature glue gun and sticks

1 Use the ribbon to make an oblong bow (see page 20) with four 4" loops, two 5" loops and two 9" tails. When wiring the bow, do not trim the wire tails. Cut the rose stem to 6" and glue it at the center of the bow, extending downward as shown.

2 Cut the pine cone pick into six 2" sprigs; glue three sprigs around the top rosebud as shown. Glue the remaining three sprigs evenly spaced among the other roses. Cut the berry stem into five 2" sprigs and glue them evenly spaced among the roses.

Floral Birdcage

3½"x5" gold-brushed burgundy metal birdcage
30" of 1/16" wide burgundy satin ribbon
1 miniature floral pick with six ½" long sprigs of yellow/burgundy/green ¼" wide silk roses with a center cluster of burgundy berries
¼ oz. of green preserved princess pine
1" long burgundy/brown mushroom bird
low temperature glue gun and sticks

1 Remove the binding from the floral pick and cut the stem of each floral sprig to ½." Glue the sprigs down the front of the birdcage, placing them in a gentle S-curve from the top left toward the center right, then back toward the bottom left as shown.

2 Use the ribbon to make a loopy bow (see page 20) with six 1½" loops and two 6" tails. Glue to the top center of the cage. Cut the princess pine into seven 1" sprigs and glue evenly spaced extending down both sides of the florals. Glue the bird to the top as shown.

Cinnamon Stick Bundle & Chipwood Box

six 5" long cinnamon sticks
34" of raffia
one 8" long sprig of cedar
one 3" long sprig of red pepper berries
low temperature glue gun and sticks

1 Hold the cinnamon sticks in a bundle and wrap the raffia around the cinnamon six times. Knot tightly to secure. Knot the raffia 2" above the first knot to form a loop. Tie the raffia ends in a shoestring bow (see page 18) with 1" loops and 2" tails.

2 Cut the cedar into 1"–3" sprigs and glue to the top center of the cinnamon bundle with the longer springs extending toward each end and the shorter sprigs on the sides. Glue the pepper berry sprig over the first raffia knot

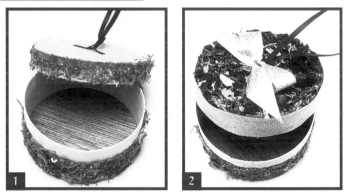

3"x1½" round chipwood box with a tightly fitting lid
18" of ⅝" wide gold lamé ribbon
9" of ⅛" wide burgundy satin ribbon
½ oz. of green dried sphagnum moss
½ oz. of burgundy/green/cream potpourri
3" of 24-gauge wire
tacky craft glue, old paintbrush

1 Crumble the moss into fine pieces. With the lid on the box, apply glue over the sides. Press the box into the moss to completely cover the sides; let dry. Fold the burgundy ribbon in half and glue the ends to the center of the lid to make a loop.

2 Cover the top of the box lid with glue and press it into the potpourri to cover. Cut a 10" piece of gold lamé ribbon and glue it around the lid side. Use the remaining gold lamé ribbon to make a collar bow (see page 21) with 1" loops and 1½" tails. Glue the bow to the center top of the lid.

Floral Bell

4" tall woven vine bell
with a 1" loop hanger
14" of ⅛" wide burgundy
twisted satin cord
5" sprig of white preserved
statice sinuata
three ½" wide burgundy
silk rosebuds
six 1" long pine cones
one 1" wide cluster of
many ⅛" wide gold
berries
¼ oz. of dark pink pre-
served ti-tree
¼ oz. of green preserved
ming fern
¼ oz. of green preserved
mini baby's breath
6" of 24-gauge wire
low temperature glue gun
and sticks

1 Cut the ming fern into 1" sprigs and glue them evenly spaced around the rim of the bell. Cut the baby's breath into ½"–¾" sprigs and glue them evenly spaced among the ming fern as shown.

2 Glue the rosebuds 3" apart around the rim of the bell. Glue one pine cone on each side of each rosebud.

3 Cut the berries into ⅛"–¼" sprigs and glue evenly around the rim of the bell. Cut the white statice into ½" sprigs and glue 1" apart around the rim some extending upward and some downward as shown.

4 Cut the ti tree into 1" sprigs and glue around the rim of the bell with the flower extending counterclockwise. Begin to make a collar bow (see page 21), but place the cord over the vine bell loop before pinching the loops together. Adjust the cord so there are 2" loops and 3" tails. Pinch and wire the bow to the vine bell loop.

Natural Packages

To make these packages, start by wrapping each in plain brown or textured paper. Grocery sacks work especially well for smaller packages. The amounts of materials used to decorate them will vary and should be in scale with the size of each package. Except for the center package, all the packages feature ribbon wrapped in both directions around the package.

1 The package at the top left is topped with a shoestring bow with no tails, then embellished with boxwood glued in a circular pattern and three 12" long crossed cinnamon sticks. Apple slices glue among the cinnamon and canella in the center finish the look.

2 A charming nest arrangement makes this package irresistable. After wrapping the ribbon and making a shoestring bow, glue a sponge mushroom to the top angled to the upper right. A small nest and terra cotta pot are glued as shown, with the pot angled over the mushroom. Tufts of moss glued around the pot and nest hide any traces of the glue. Glue barly heads extending down to the left, 3" cinnamon sprigs in the pot and plumoses

fern sprigs evenly around the pot. Two mushroom birds area a nice final touch.

3 This corrugated-paper-wrapped gift gets its country charm from the gingham ribbon, finished in a four loop puffy bow. Three parchment roses glued are to the center of the bow for a pretty touch. Two raspberry sprigs are glued extending toward opposite corners on the package. Cedar sprigs and dried artemesia are glued evenly among all the components.

4 The center package uses the floral technique, pavé. Nigella, pinecones and dried fruits are glued to the package in diagonal rows, all separated by cinnamon sticks. Glue a ribbon around the sides of the package.

5 A premade pick containing pods, holy leaves and pine sprigs was glued over the birch printed paper ribbon on this woodsy package. Instead of a bow, twigs were clipped from the back of a grapevine wreath and wrapped over the pick with the ends glued to the package to secure.

Fancy Packages

These elegant packages are simple to do. All are wrapped in white paper, then have ribbon wrapped over the top, crossed in back, brought to the top again over the opposite sides and tied to secure.

1 An oblong bow with four loops tops this package. To finish the package, a stem of silk magnolias with leaves and berries attached is glued to the center of the bow extending down the length of the gift.

2 This sweet little gift features a poinsettia with berries and leaves glued in place, nicely replacing the need for a bow. A few sprigs of dried ti tree were added around the flower for texture.

3 Before wrapping, cut the paper to size, then take it outside and lay it on a section of newspaper. Spray short bursts of burgundy paint from a spray can, applying it lightly and evenly over the surface to give the paper a speckled look. Multiple colors can be used for different effects. Let the paper dry completely, then wrap the gift with it. Lay a crocheted doily on the top of the gift before wrapping the gift with ribbon. Glue preserved cedar, German statice and a silk rose in the same tones as the paint in a diagonal line across the fit to add the finishing touches.

4 This gift starts with the wrapped ribbon technique, but tails are left to extend toward the corners of the gift. Cut an inverted "V" at each end. Tie a length of ribbon around the center knot to form two more tails and cut the ends as before. Glue a large silk rose to the center of the package, covering the knot. Accent the rose by gluing latex leaves, berries and smaller silk flowers around it. Add two stand-up bows in thin gold ribbon to opposite sides of the rose, finishing the package.

Fabulous & Fresh Boughs & Bows

Nothing evokes a feeling of the Christmas season like the scent of fresh pine, fir and cedar during the holidays. Bringing greens into the home, like wreaths, was originally done to lift the spirits during the long winter months and remind people that spring was just around the corner.

The greens used in these projects were gathered from forests and back yards here in the Pacific Northwest. However, because those types may not grow in your area, simply gather greenery which is indigenous to your location and substitute those types for what is listed in the projects.

Wreaths, swags and centerpieces created from fresh greenery sprigs and branches provide the scents as well as beautiful decorations and festive touches to a home. Berries, twig bells, pheasant feathers, pine cones and pods all decorate pieces with a natural or woodsy feeling.

The Silvered Centerpiece on page 128 is done in tones of silver and white with the greenery as a backdrop, which produces an elegant design. Another opulent piece is the Vertical Swag on page 130. It features gilded burgundy roses and gold berries on cedar and pine boughs, then is enhanced with an elegant ribbon and twisted cording, pulling all the colors together.

With the correct tools, fresh greenery is easy to work with and can last the entire Christmas season, providing wonderful scents and distinctive decorations throughout the home.

Tips & Techniques with Greens

While fresh greenery can be constructed into spectacular designs, the following tips can help provide long-lasting, beautiful pieces to be displayed either in the home or outside the door to welcome guests. With care, fresh designs should last for several weeks if displayed inside a home and for months if displayed outside.

The main element to remember when making decorations from fresh greens is to pull the wire tightly during construction. As the greens dry, the stems and branches will begin to shrink and loose wiring will allow the branches to fall out.

Any combination of materials can be used indoors, but if the piece is to be displayed outside, here are a few tips to make sure it remains beautiful the entire Christmas season.

Latex flowers will weather the outdoor elements the best, followed by silks. Dried flowers, while generally not durable enough to be used outside, should hold their color and shape long enough for a seasonal display, especially on a covered porch or veranda.

Plastic or metallic ribbon is the best choice for outdoor use, and wire-edged ribbon will hold its shape nicely and add a richness to the design.

Holiday picks are terrific elements for fresh arrangements and decorations. They add color, shine and unusual shapes to greenery designs.

Red Berry Wreath

9" wide wire wreath ring

2¼ yards of 3" wide red/green/gold plaid ribbon with gold wired edges

seventy 5"–7" long fresh fir boughs (noble, grand and Douglas used here)

3 stems of red latex frosted berries, each with three 3"–4" wide clusters of many ½" wide berries, some frosted

3 red latex berry picks, each with six ¾" wide berries

1 stem of green latex holly with 4 clusters of many ¼" wide berries and many 1"–3" long leaves

three 4" long pine cones

3 holiday picks, each with three ½" wide red foil wrapped gifts

1 paddle of 20-gauge wire

low temperature glue gun and sticks

1 Lay the ring on a flat surface. Attach the end of the wire to the wreath frame (the paddle should be on the inside of the ring). Lay two fir boughs on the ring, extending left and center and wrap the wire around the stems. Lay two more boughs on the ring, extending right and center and wrap with the wire. Continue, overlapping the previous stems and alternating the types of bough until the ring is completely covered. Trim the excess wire to 8" and twist at the back to make a wreath hanger (see page 12).

2 Wire the pine cones evenly spaced around the wreath. Cut the frosted berries into nine 4" sprigs and glue them to the wreath, evenly spaced, leaving the lower area between 7:00 to 4:00 empty.

3 Glue the berry picks evenly spaced around the wreath. Cut the holly into four 5" sprigs with berries and leaves and seven 3" individual leaf sprigs; glue them evenly spaced around the wreath.

4 Glue the holiday picks evenly among the floral area. Use the ribbon to make an oblong bow (see page 20) with a center loop, two 4" loops, four 5" loops and two 9" tails. Glue the bow to the wreath at 6:00.

Hurricane Lamp Centerpiece

1 glass hurricane lamp with an 8" tall
   chimney and 6" round dish
2½ yards of 1" wide red/green/black plaid
   taffeta ribbon
thirty 8" long boughs of fresh cedar
twelve 6" long boughs of bloomed incense
   cedar
ten 4" long sprigs of blueberry juniper
ten 2" long pine cones
6 red apple picks, each with a 1" wide
   apple, two ½" wide apple quarters and
   two 1" wide variegated holly leaves
4"x 4"x4" block of floral foam for fresh
   materials
12" tall red taper candle
low temperature glue gun and sticks

1 Soak the foam in water until it is thoroughly
   saturated. Push the support bar of the lamp
into the center of the foam until it fits into the
dish at the lamp base. Fill the dish with water.

2 Insert the longest cedar sprigs around the lower
   perimeter of the foam. Continue working
around the foam adding the shorter pieces, angling
the cedar upward. Insert the incense cedar evenly
spaced as shown.

3 Insert four sprigs of juniper around the base of
   the support bar, angled upward. Insert the
remaining juniper evenly spaced around the base,
2" from cedar sprigs. Glue the pine cones throughout the greenery as shown.

4 Cut the ribbon into two equal lengths and use
   each to make an oblong bow (see page 20)
with a center loop, two 2" loops, two 3" loops and
two 8" tails. Trim the tails diagonally. Glue one
bow to each side of the centerpiece at the base of
the support bar. Glue the apple picks evenly spaced
among the greenery as shown. Place the candle in
the holder.

Wreath with Pheasant Feathers

9" wide wire wreath ring
approximately forty 7" long fresh noble fir boughs
approximately forty 7" long fresh cedar boughs
three 12" long fresh cedar boughs
1 stem of red silk poinsettias with two 6" wide
   and one 3" wide blossom
3 red latex berry picks, each with six ¾" wide
   berries
2 oz. of green preserved mahonia
three 1½"–2½" long pine cones
3 oz. of dried barley
2 oz. of dried brisa media
six 12"–14" long
   pheasant feathers
1 paddle of 22-
   gauge wire
low temperature
   glue gun and
   sticks

1 Lay the ring on a flat surface. Attach one end of the wire to the wreath frame. Without cutting the wire, hold three fir boughs against the ring and wrap the wire tightly around the stems 3–4 times to secure. Hold two boughs of cedar against the ring and wrap the wire tightly again. Repeat to cover the entire ring.

2 Loop two feathers in half and wire the ends together. Glue the looped feathers to the wreath at 8:00 as shown. Glue four feathers to the left of the looped feathers, two extending up and two extending down as shown. Cut the mahonia into two 8" sprigs and four 6" sprigs. Glue one 8" sprig between the upper feathers and one 8" sprig above the feather at the lower right. Glue the 6" sprigs evenly spaced around the looped feathers.

3 Cut the poinsettias into three 3" sprigs and glue them in a triangular pattern at 8:00. Glue the pine cones in a triangular pattern between the poinsettias.

4 Cut the barley into 6" sprigs and wire them together in clusters of three; glue the clusters and berry picks evenly spaced around the poinsettias as shown. Cut the brisa media into 7" sprigs and glue them evenly spaced among the florals. Glue the 12" cedar boughs behind the florals at 8:00, extending downward. Attach a wire hanger (see page 12) at the top back.

Country Garland

approximately 150 boughs of fresh cedar, each 8" long
twenty 8" long boughs of fresh white pine
5½ yards of burgundy/blue plaid ribbon with wired
  edges
4 stems of white anemone, each with two 3" wide
  blossoms and three 1" wide buds

3 oz. of burgundy preserved heather
2 oz. of dark blue dried larkspur
2 oz. of dried avena
3 oz. of dried bloom broom
one paddle of 22-gauge wire
low temperature glue gun and sticks

1 Hold three cedar boughs and twist the wire 3–4 times tightly 3" from the ends of the stems. Without cutting the wire, overlap three more cedar boughs with the stem ends 1" higher than the first bundle and repeat. Continue overlapping and wrapping, adding a pine bough every 8" until the garland is 60" long. Break a few small cedar sprigs off the longer boughs and wire to the beginning of the garland to cover the exposed wire.

2 Cut six 6" ribbon lengths and trim the ends diagonally. Set aside for step 4. Cut the remaining ribbon in half. With each half, make an oblong bow (see page 20) with a center loop, two 3½ loops, four 5" loops and two 10" tails. Glue the bows 6" from each end of the garland. Cut the anemone stems to 5" and glue them evenly spaced among the greenery between the bows.

3 Cut the heather into 5" sprigs. Glue two or three pieces around each bow, angled toward the end as shown. Glue the remaining sprigs evenly spaced among the florals. Cut the larkspur into 5" pieces and glue them evenly spaced among the florals and greenery.

4 Pinch and wire the straight end of each ribbon length from step 2. Glue them evenly spaced among the greenery. Cut the avena into 6" sprigs and glue them evenly spaced among the florals, angled toward the bottom of the garland. Cut the bloom broom into 5" sprigs. Wire them together in 2"–3" wide clusters, then glue them evenly spaced among the florals; glue one sprig on each side of each bow. Attach a wire hanger (see page 12) at the top back and each end.

Velvet Poinsettia Swag

six 20"–30" fresh cedar boughs

3½ yards of burgundy/green/gold tapestry ribbon with gold wired edges

3 stems of burgundy velvet poinsettias, each with one 7" wide blossom

2 stems of gold silk roses, each with five 1" wide blossoms and seven 1" long leaves

1 stem of burgundy silk heather with three 7" long branches of many blossom sprigs

2 stems of green latex mum leaves, each with 1 section of 8 and 2 sections of six 2" long leaves

2 oz. of dried rice grass

22-gauge wire

low temperature glue gun and sticks

1 Lay the cedar boughs on a flat surface with the longer branches toward the back, and the shorter branches at the front, angled toward the outside. Hold all the bough stems together and wire them securely. Twist the wire at the back to form a hanger (see page 12).

2 Use the ribbon to make a puffy bow (see page 20) with six 7" loops and two 20" tails. Trim the tails diagonally and glue the bow to the swag over the stems. Cut the poinsettia stems to 2" and glue one at the bow center, one right and one left of the bow as shown.

3 Cut each gold rose stem to 10"; glue one below the bow, angled downward left and one above the bow, angled upward right. Cut the heather into three 8" sprigs; glue one extending from under each outer poinsettia, angled downward and one extending from below the center poinsettia.

4 Cut the leaves into two 8" and four 6" sprigs. Glue one 8" sprig above and right of the center poinsettia, and one above and right of it. Glue the rest evenly around all the poinsettias. Cut the rice grass into 7" sprigs and glue them evenly spaced among the florals.

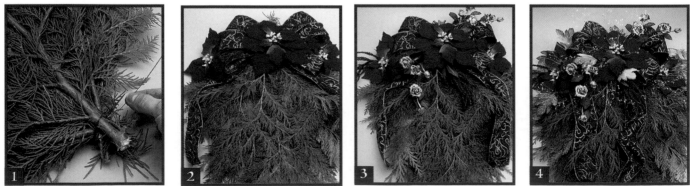

Holiday Greens Wreath

9" wide wire wreath ring
approximately sixty 5"–7" long
   fresh noble fir boughs
fifteen 5"–7" long blueberry juniper
   boughs
fifteen 6"–8" long incense cedar
   boughs
ten 5" long holly boughs
three 4" long pine cones
3 red latex berry picks, each with six
   ¾" wide berries
1 paddle of 20-gauge wire
low temperature glue gun and sticks

1 Lay the ring on a flat surface. Attach one end of the wire to the wreath frame. Lay two fir boughs over the ring, one extending out and the other extending up to cover the ring. Wrap the wire around these boughs 2–3 times and pull it tight. Place two more fir boughs on the ring, extending inward and center, then wrap them with the wire. Repeat to finish one-third of the area around the ring.

2 Lay two incense cedar boughs and two blueberry juniper boughs together on the ring as shown and wrap with the wire. Continue with more fir. At the two-thirds point around the ring, wrap cedar and juniper onto the wreath. Continue with more fir until you are almost at the starting point. Finish by attaching the cedar and juniper.

There should be three areas of cedar and juniper evenly spaced around the wreath. Trim the excess wire to 8" and twist to make a wreath hanger (see page 12).

3 Wrap a 10" length of wire around the base of a pine cone. Wire the cone to the wreath midway between two areas of cedar and juniper. Repeat with the remaining pine cones, spacing them evenly around the wreath between the groups of cedar and juniper.

4 Glue one berry pick near each pine cone. Glue the holly sprigs evenly spaced around the wreath.

Silvered Centerpiece

9" round white ceramic bowl
thirty 5"–10" long fresh noble fir boughs
1 ⅓ yards of 1 ½" wide sheer silver ribbon with wired edges
3 stems of white silk carnations, each with three 10" long sections of one 1" wide blossom
3 stems of white silk vervain, each with three 7" long blossom clusters
3 oz. of silver preserved holly
2 oz. of dried birch twigs
5" x 5" square of floral foam for fresh materials
one 8" tall white pillar candle
silver spray paint
newspapers
waterproof tape

1 Lay the birch twigs on the newspaper and spray with the silver paint. Let dry. Soak the foam in water until it is thoroughly saturated. Place the foam in the center of the bowl. Attach a strip of waterproof tape across the foam diagonally, securing it to both sides of the bowl. Fill the bowl with water. Insert the fir into the foam to form an oval shape as shown (be careful not to pull on the fir once it has been inserted, as it will tear the foam). Insert the longer boughs around the base and add shorter sprigs when moving upward around the foam. Leave a 3" area in the center of the foam empty for the candle.

2 Cut the carnations into nine 8" sprigs and insert them into the foam, evenly spaced among the fir. Cut the vervain into nine 7" sprigs and insert them as for the carnations, curving the blossoms downward.

3 Cut two 12" ribbon lengths. Wire one end of each length and insert the wired ends

into the left end of the foam as shown. With the remaining ribbon, make a standup bow (see page 19) with four 3" loops. Insert the wired end of the bow into the right end of the foam, opposite the tails. Cut the birch twigs into 10" sprigs and insert them in clusters at the corners of the centerpiece as shown.

4 Cut the holly into 6" sprigs and insert them into the foam, evenly spaced among the fir. Place the candle in the center of the design.

Swag with Twig Bells

boughs of fresh noble fir: three 24" long and one 36" long

two 5" long twig bells

4⅔ yards of 3½" wide red/green holiday print ribbon with gold wired edges

two 3" long pine cones

5 gift picks, each with three 1" wide red foil-wrapped gifts

2 stems of red berries, each with five 10" long sections of many ¼" wide teardrop-shaped berries

22-gauge wire

low temperature glue gun and sticks

1 Hold the fir boughs together with the 36" bough in the back, angled downward and the 24" boughs in front, one angled down and the others slightly to the right and left. Wire the stems of the boughs together securely. Twist the end of the wire into a hanger (see page 12) at the back of the swag.

2 With the ribbon, make an oblong bow (see page 20) with a center loop, six 5" loops, two 7" loops, four 10" and two 15" tails. Cut the tails in an inverted "V." Glue the bow at the top of the swag; angle the tails as shown. Clip three 4" fir sprigs from the back of the swag and glue them evenly spaced among the bow loops.

3 Hold the bells together, one bell 2" above the other and wire them together. Glue them below the center of the bow. Glue one pine cone to the right of the bow and one above the bow.

4 Glue the gift picks to the swag evenly spaced around the bow and among the loops as shown. Cut the red berries into nine 5"–9" sprigs and two 2" sprigs. Glue a 2" sprig into each bell. Glue the remaining berry sprigs evenly around the bow, positioning the longer sprigs around the lower area and the shorter sprigs around the top and sides.

Vertical Garland

approximately 200 boughs of fresh cedar, each 8" long

thirty 8" boughs of fresh white pine

2¾ yards of 4" wide green/burgundy/gold striped ribbon with wired edges

3 yards of ½" wide red/gold twisted cord

5 stems of gold-edged burgundy silk roses, each with one 4" wide blossom

2 stems of green latex rose leaves, each with twenty 1"–2" long leaves

2 stems of burgundy latex skimmia, each with three 2" wide clusters of many berries

2 stems of gold latex mini berries, each with nine sprigs of three 1" wide clusters of many berries

2 stems of purple latex grapes, each with three 4" wide clusters of many ½" wide grapes

five 3"–4" wide dried lotus pods

4 oz. of brown preserved spiral eucalyptus

1 paddle of 22-gauge wire

low temperature glue gun and sticks

1 Hold three cedar boughs; twist the wire tightly 3" from the ends of the stems. Without cutting the wire, overlap three more cedar boughs with the stem ends 1" away from the stems of the first bundle and repeat. Continue overlapping and wrapping, adding a pine bough every 8" until the garland is 72" long.

2 Use the ribbon to make an oblong bow (see page 20) with a center loop, four 4" loops, four 5½" loops and two 8" tails. Glue the bow to the stem end of the garland, as shown. Make a 3" loop at one end of the cord and wire it behind the bow at the back to form a hanger. Wrap the cord spiral fashion around the garland to the other end; glue every wrap at the back to secure. Cut the roses into 4" sprigs and glue them evenly spaced down the garland, alternately angling them from side to side.

3 Cut the lotus pods to 4" long and glue them as for the roses. Cut the rose leaves into 6" sprigs and glue them evenly among the greenery as shown. Cut the eucalyptus into 5" sprigs and glue them evenly spaced among the greenery in clusters of 2–3 sprigs.

4 Cut the skimmia into four 4" and two 2" sprigs. Cut the grapes into six 4" sprigs and the gold mini berries into eighteen 3" sprigs. Glue all the sprigs evenly spaced among the florals.

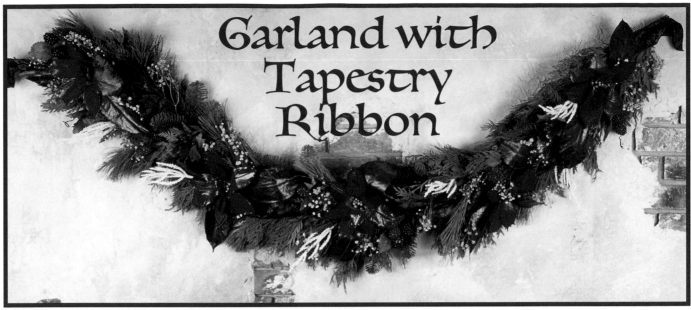

Garland with Tapestry Ribbon

approximately 150 boughs of fresh
   cedar, each 7" long
twenty 8" long boughs of fresh white
   pine
forty 8" long boughs of fresh noble fir
2½ yards of 2¾" wide red/green floral
   tapestry ribbon
5 stems of red latex poinsettias, each
   with one 7" wide blossom and two 6"
   long leaves

2 stems of red/burgundy latex raspberries, each with seven 1½" wide berries
2 stems of white latex heather, each with
   three 7" long sprigs of many branched
   blossom clusters
1 stem of green latex holly with four
   clusters of six ¼" wide berries and
   many 1"–2" long leaves
4 oz. of preserved baby's breath
22-gauge paddle wire
low temperature glue gun and sticks

1 Hold three cedar boughs; attach the wire 3" from the ends of the stems and wrap together. Without cutting the wire, overlap two more cedar boughs and a sprig of fir with the stem ends 1" away from the stems of the first bundle and wrap with wire. Continue overlapping and wrapping, alternating cedar alone with cedar and fir and adding a pine sprig every 8", until the garland is 72" long. Break a few small cedar sprigs off the longer boughs and wire to the beginning of the garland to cover the exposed wire. At each end, attach a wire hanger (see page 12) on the back.

2 Weave the ribbon through the greenery as shown and glue at each end to secure. Cut the poinsettias to 3" long; glue them evenly spaced among the greenery. Cut the leaves from the poinsettia stems and glue two near each flower.

3 Cut the raspberry stems into six 4" sprigs and glue them in a staggered pattern among the greenery, alternately angling them to each side of the garland. Cut the heather into six 7" sprigs and glue them as for the raspberries.

4 Cut the holly into four 5" sprigs, each with one berry cluster, and seven 3" sprigs of individual leaves. Glue the sprigs with berries between the poinsettias and use the leaves to fill any empty areas. Cut the baby's breath into 4" sprigs and glue them evenly among the florals in clusters of three sprigs as shown.

Fast, Easy &
FESTIVE

As Christmas draws near, extra time becomes scarce and precious. The season is brimming with fun activities too good to miss. We're here to help: this section is filled with designs which can be completed in an hour or less.

The Speedy Magnolia Swag on page 137 features combining a green pine swag with a magnolia swag, creating a very stunning and elegant piece to be hang over a window, doorway or fireplace. By using those two "almost finsihed" components, very little is needed to complete a wonderful design.

Garlands of pine or fir are very versatile and can quickly be made into elaborate decorations for bookcases, as the Mini Swags on page 142 prove. The Twin corners on page 143 also began as one long garland. Because the garlands contain so many pine sprigs and have a flexible, yet sturdy base, creating these splendid corners becomes a simple matter of adding floral materials and bows. What could be simpler, yet produce such a lovely effect?

These beautiful and clever designs were created with the person who has very little time, yet wants wonderful decorations for the home or to give as gifts.

Gilded Centerpiece & Poinsettia Wreath

two stems of vinyl pine, each with a 22" section of
twenty-four 5" long sprigs

2 3/4 yards of 2 1/2" wide burgundy/gold brocade ribbon
with wired edges

2 latex peony picks, each with a 6" and 3" wide red
blossom, a 2" wide gold bud, a cluster of nine 1/2"
grapes and many 2"–6" long leaves

2 oz. of 6"–8" long birch twigs

four 3" wide gold ball ornaments

metallic gold spray paint, newspapers

12" of 24-gauge wire

low temperature glue gun and sticks

1 Place the twigs on newspaper, spray them with
gold paint and let dry. Overlap the two pine
stems to form a 32" long swag centerpiece and wire
together to secure. Wire the two peony picks
together to form a 26" long swag and wire it to the
center of the pine centerpiece.

2 With the ribbon, make an oblong bow (see
page 20) with a center loop, two 3" loops, two
4" loops, two 6" loops and two 18" tails. Glue to
the center of the centerpiece and arrange the tails
among the peonies as shown in large photo. Cut
the twigs to 6"–8" long and glue them evenly
among the pine. Glue a ball ornament on each side
of the bow and one on each end of the centerpiece.

one 16" grapevine wreath

1 3/4 yards of 2 1/2" wide burgundy/gold brocade ribbon
with wired edges

2 stems of vinyl pine, each with a 12" section of twelve
5" long sprigs

1 stem of gold gilded burgundy latex poinsettia with one
8" wide blossom and two 5" long shiny, glittered
leaves

2 gold latex berry picks, each with a cluster of twelve 1/2"
berries and three 2" long leaves

2 gift picks, each with a 1" wide gold gift, 1" wide gold
apple, two 3" sprigs of many 1/2" gold leaves, one 2"
long glittered pine cone, three 2" long pine and three
2 1/2" long silk leaves

2 stems of gold plastic coral, each with three 4"–7" long
branches of many sprigs

12" of 24-gauge wire

low temperature glue gun and sticks

1 Cut the pine stems to 12" and glue them to
the wreath with the stems ends touching at
9:00. Curve the picks to follow the shape of the
wreath. With the ribbon, make a standup bow (see
page 19) with four 4" loops and two 16" tails. Glue
at 9:00 and arrange tails as shown.

2 Cut the stem off the poinsettia and glue the
blossom just inside the bow. Glue the leaves at
7:00 and 8:00. Glue a gift pick above and one
below the poinsettia. Glue a berry pick above and
one below the bow as shown. Cut the coral into six
4"–7" sprigs and glue evenly among the greenery.
Attach a wire hanger (see page 12).

Frosted Centerpiece

2 stems of frosted pine, each with an 18" section of many 3" pine sprigs, four 2"–5" long frosted cones, 4 sprigs of 4"–9" long white frosted coral and many 3"–4" long frosted ivy leaves
2 stems of red latex berries, each with five clusters of seven ½" berries and two 1½" long leaves
3 taper candle cups
three 12" long red taper candles
one 2"x 6" piece of floral foam for drieds
serrated knife
24-gauge wire, low temperature glue gun and sticks

1 Position the two pine stems end to end overlapping the stems and wire together to secure. Cut the foam into three 2" cubes and gently push a candle cup into the center of each as shown.

2 Glue a foam piece in the center of the swag and one 8" away each side of it. Cut the berry stem into ten 2"–3" sprigs and glue them evenly throughout the centerpiece as shown. Insert a candle into each cup.

Frosted Door Hanger

one 11"x19" semicircular twig wall plaque
1 ¾ yards of 3" wide red metallic open weave wire ribbon
one 18" long stem of frosted pine with many 3" long pine sprigs, five 2"–5" long frosted cones, four 5"–8" long sprigs of white frosted coral and many 2"–4" long frosted ivy leaves
1 stem of red latex berries with 6 sprigs of many ¼" berries
textured "snow" paint, #10 flat paintbrush
24-gauge wire, low temperature glue gun and sticks

1 Use the textured snow to paint the wall plaque white. Let dry. Attach the frosted wall plaque to the arch by bending the stem over the center of the twig frame as shown. Secure with glue.

2 With the ribbon, make a stand up bow (see page 19) with seven 6" loops. Glue it to the arch at the top of the frosted swag. Cut the berry stem into six 4"–7" sprigs and glue evenly among the frosted pine, angled as shown.

Place Card Holders & Napkin Rings

FOR EACH SET:
red/green plaid, green and white paper, pen to write name
1 linen napkin
decorative scissors
low temperature glue gun and sticks

FOR ONE RED & GREEN SET:
one 4" wide vinyl pine wreath
1 yard of ½" wide red satin ribbon
two holiday picks, each with one ¾" long apple, two ¾" apple slices and five 1"–2" long holly leaves

FOR ONE SILVER SET:
one 4" wide grapevine wreath
24" of 6mm silver fused beads
12" of ½" wide silver ribbon
2 holiday picks, each with 1" wide silver package, 1¼" wide silver ball, 1" wide silver apple, 2 clusters of many ¼" silver berries, ⅜" wide silver ribbon and two 2½" long silver leaves

Whether red and green or silver tones, each set is constructed in the same manner. This makes it easy to match your own decor.

1 If you are using a pine wreath, fluff the sprigs. Cut a 24" length of ribbon. Wind it around the wreath; glue the ends to the back.

2 Glue a pick one side of the wreath as shown. Cut a 1½"x4" piece of plaid paper. Mat it on a piece of green paper cut with decorative scissors. Place a ½"x 3" piece of white paper cut with decorative scissors in the middle of the plaid piece to hand letter a name on. Tuck this place card into the wreath.

3 Fold the remaining ribbon in half. Snip a ⅛" incision on the fold. Trim the ends of the ribbon diagonally. Cut the pick stem to ¼".

4 Insert the pick through the incision in the ribbon and glue at the back to secure. Tie the ribbon around the napkin with the pick on top and a shoestring bow (see page 18) with two 1½" loops and 3" tails underneath. Repeat steps 1-4 for each set of holders and rings.

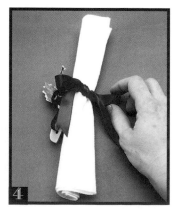

Speedy Magnolia Swag

one 36" long green vinyl pine swag with ten 1"–3" long cones and many 5"–9"long pine sprigs

1 ½ yards of 3" wide gold sheer ribbon with wired edges

one 30" long silk magnolia swag with three 7" wide white blossoms, 2 buds and twenty-four 4"–6" long green leaves

2 stems of ivory latex grapes, each with three 2"–4" long clusters of many ½" grapes and ten 1"–1 ½" long leaves

2 stems of gold latex coral each with three 6" long branches of many sprigs

24-gauge wire

low temperature glue gun and sticks

1 Fluff the branches of the pine swag. Center the magnolia swag over the pine swag and wire together under each magnolia to secure. Add a wire hanger (see page 12) to the center back.

2 Glue one of the stems of ivory grapes to the lower right of the center magnolia, extending right. Glue the other stem of grapes to the upper left of the center magnolia, extending left.

3 Cut the coral into six 6" sprigs. Glue one to the upper right and one to the lower left of the center magnolia, angled as shown. Glue one above and one below each outer magnolia, angled toward the swag ends.

4 Weave the ribbon gently among the greenery and magnolias from left to right as shown. Glue at the center and at each end to secure.

Cedar Pine Cone Basket

one 12"x 8" flat backed wood slat basket with 7" tall handle
2 yards of 2½" wide blue/green/burgundy plaid striped ribbon with wired edges
2 stems of burgundy latex raspberries, each with 2 clusters of five ½" berries and four 1½" long leaves
6 oz. of green preserved cedar
2 oz. of dark blue dried holly
ten 4"–6" long pine cones
24-gauge wire
low temperature glue gun and sticks

1 Glue the 10" sprigs extending from the left handle base up the handle and forward along the basket rim. Glue the shorter sprigs to fill the area over the stems of the 10" sprigs.

2 Cut the berries into four 5" sprigs. Glue three to the cedar at the handle base, one extending upward, one to the left and one toward the front of the basket. Glue the last sprig in front of the sprig that extends forward, angled down over the front of the basket.

3 With the ribbon, make a puffy bow (see page 20) with a center loop, six 3½" loops, a 9" tail and a 17" tail. Glue the bow to the cedar at the handle base and glue the 9" tail along the back rim of the basket. Angle the 17" tail down the front of the basket as shown and glue.

4 Cut the holly into 3"–4" sprigs and glue them evenly among the cedar. Angle the sprigs above the bow upward and the sprigs below the bow forward. Attach a wire hanger (see page 12) to the center top of the basket back. Fill the basket with the pine cones.

Potpourri Vase

one 3"x7 1/2" glass cylinder vase
6 oz. package burgundy/green potpourri
3 stems of gold-brushed burgundy silk roses, each
 with one 5" wide blossom
1 stem of green latex rose leaves with twenty-one
 1 1/2" long leaves
2 stems of ivory silk vervain, each with three 7"
 long blossom sprigs
1 stem of gold latex mini-berries with nine 4"
 sprigs of three 1" wide clusters of many 1/8"
 berries
1 stem of burgundy latex grapes with three 3 1/2"
 long clusters of many 1/2" grapes and five 1"
 long leaves
4 oz. of green preserved cedar
low temperature glue gun and sticks

1 Open the package of potpourri and slowly shake it into the vase. Lightly
pack it and add more until the vase is full. The potpourri must not be
packed too tightly or it will be difficult to insert the floral stems into the vase.

2 Cut one rose stem to 10" and the other two to 7". Insert the long rose
into the back center of the vase until the head is 7" above the vase rim.
Insert one rose to the right and one to the left of the first stem until the blossoms are just above vase rim. Cut the cedar into 6"–12" sprigs and glue them
evenly among the roses with the longer sprigs toward the back.

3 Cut the rose leaves into one 10" sprig with six leaves and five 5" sprigs,
each with three leaves. Glue the 10" sprig behind the 10" rose. Glue the
5" sprigs evenly among the cedar and roses. Cut the vervain into six 7" sprigs
and glue them as near materials of similar lengths, gently curving the sprigs.

4 Cut the gold mini berry into nine 4" sprigs with three berry clusters each.
Glue them evenly spaced among the florals and greenery. Cut each grape
cluster with a 1/2" stem and glue one between the lower roses, angled downward. Glue one grape sprig above each of the lower roses, angled toward the outside as shown.

Tri-Corner Swag

50" long green vinyl pine garland

3 ¼ yards of 1 ½" wide red/gold/green striped grosgrain ribbon with wired edges

2 stems of white silk roses, each with 4 clusters of two 1 ½" wide blossoms, 1 bud and four 1 ½" long leaves

1 green silk holly bush with ten sprigs of five 1"–3" long leaves and one cluster of many ¼" red berries

sixteen 2" long pine cones

24-gauge wire

low temperature glue gun and sticks

1 Fluff the garland and cut into two sections, one 30" and one 20". Bend the 30" section in half to form a 90° angle. Wire the 20" section to the corner of the bent section, extending downward to form a T-shape as shown.

2 Cut a 30" and a 42" length of ribbon and trim the ends diagonally. Weave the 42" section among the pine branches across the top of the "T" from end to end. Glue the ends to secure. Weave the 30" section of ribbon in the vertical section of garland and glue the ends to secure. With the remaining ribbon, make an oblong bow (see page 20) with a center loop, two 3" loops, two 3½" loops and two 4" loops. Glue it to the center of the "T" where the two sections of garland meet.

3 Cut the roses into eight 4" sprigs and glue them evenly spaced among all the pine sprigs, with five sprigs across the top and three down the lower section as shown. Cut the holly into ten 4" sprigs and glue them evenly among all the pine.

4 Glue the pine cones evenly among the pine as shown. Attach wire hangers (see page 12) at the top left, right and center of the swag.

Bow Swag

one 18" long green vinyl pine garland with many 6"
   long sprigs
3 yards of 4" wide burgundy/green/gold striped ribbon
   with wired edges
one 12" long poinsettia pick with a 7" wide burgundy
   blossom, a 1½" wide apple, three ¾" berries and
   eight 2"–4" long holly leaves
2 oz. of green preserved cedar
1 stem of burgundy latex skimmia with two 3" and one
   1½" long clusters of many 1⁄16" berries and nine 2"
   long leaves
2 oz. of white preserved heather
six 1½" wide wood star cutouts
metallic gold spray paint
newspapers
12" of 24-gauge wire
low temperature glue gun and sticks

1 Use the ribbon to make a puffy bow (see page
19) with five 7" loops and two 16" tails. Fluff
the pine garland and wire one end to the bow center as shown. Glue to reinforce. Attach a wire
hanger (see page 12) to the center back of the bow.

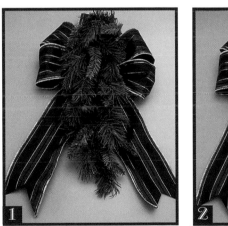

2 Cut the cedar into 4"–6" sprigs and glue
them evenly among the pine branches,
angled downward. Glue the poinsettia pick to
the pine garland with the blossom at the center
of the bow and the leaves and fruit angled
downward.

3 Place the stars on the newspaper and spray
gold; allow them to dry completely. Glue
them evenly among the floral area as shown
with three around the poinsettia blossom and
three toward extending down the garland.

4 Cut the skimmia into three 4"–5"
sprigs, each with a clump of berries
and 2–4 leaves. Glue one of the large
clusters below and right of the poinsettia and the other large cluster to the
garland, angled left about 4" below the
poinsettia blossom. Glue the small
cluster at the center of the garland, just
below the end of the poinsettia pick.
Cut the heather into 3"–4" sprigs and
glue them evenly among the floral area,
angled outward around the bow and
downward among the pine sprigs.

Mini Swags

one 30" long green vinyl pine garland with many 3"–4" pine sprigs
2½ yards of 1½" wide green satin ribbon with a ¾" wide vertical stripe of red poinsettias
1 stem of white silk roses with 2 sprigs of two 1½" wide blossoms; 4 sprigs of a 1½" blossom and a ¾" bud and six 1½" long leaves
1 stem of red latex mini-berries with 9 sprigs of three 2" wide clusters of many ⅛" berries and two ½" long leaves
2 stems of gold latex berries, each with six sprigs of five ½" berries
2 oz. of green preserved plumosus fern
2 oz. of preserved rice grass
low temperature glue gun and sticks

1 Cut the section of garland in half and fluff the branches to extend toward both ends from the center. With the ribbon make two puffy bows (see page 20), each with a center loop, four 3" loops and two 9" tails. Glue a bow in the center of each garland section. Wind one ribbon tail toward each end of the swag and glue to secure.

2 Cut the rose stem into eight 3"–5" sprigs, four with one blossom and four with one blossom and a bud. Glue a single one blossom above and one below each bow on each swag. Glue remaining sprigs to the swags, one at each end of each swag.

3 Cut the red mini berry into nine 4" sprigs, each with three clusters of berries. Glue all but one to the swags, two on each side of the bow, spaced as shown. Cut the last sprig into two sprigs and glue one to each swag above the bow. Cut the plumosus into 4" sprigs and glue them evenly among the pine sprigs.

4 Cut the gold berries into twelve 4" sprigs with five berries each. Glue six evenly spaced to each swag. Cut the rice grass into 4" sprigs and glue them evenly to each swag around the bow and among the pine sprigs.

Twin Corners

one 5' long green vinyl pine garland
5 yards of 1½" wide green/black/red plaid ribbon with
   wired edges
6 grape picks, each with ten ¼"–½" purple grapes and
   three 2"–3" long leaves
ten 2" long pine cones

3 oz. of dried barley
6 oz. of red dried pepper berries
2 oz. of green dried silene grass
2 oz. of dried black lichen
30-gauge wire
low temperature glue gun and sticks

1 Fluff the garland and cut in half. Bend the swag in the middle to form a 90° angle. Cut the ribbon in half and trim the ends diagonally. Make two puffy bows (see page 20), with a center loop, six 4" loops and two 20" tails. Glue a bow to each swag corner. Arrange the tails with one extending toward each end, gluing to secure.

2 Glue three grape picks to each swag, with one at the center extending from the bow and one near each end as shown. Glue five pine cones to each swag evenly spaced among the greenery.

3 Cut the barley into 4" sprigs and glue half among the picks and ribbon of each swag, alternating toward the outside and inside as shown. Cut the pepper berries into 3" sprigs and repeat.

4 Cut the silene grass into 4" sprigs and glue half evenly spaced among the sprigs of each swag, alternating toward the outside and inside. Break the lichen into 2" tufts and glue to fill empty areas. Attach a wire hanger (see page 12) to each end of the vertical sections.

INDEX